GCSE Design

Food technology

Lesley Woods

Series Editor: Geoff Hancock

www.heinemann.co.uk
✓ Free online support
✓ Useful weblinks
✓ 24 hour online ordering

01865 888058

Inspiring generations

Heinemann Educational Publishers
Halley Court, Jordan Hill, Oxford, OX2 8EJ
Part of Harcourt Education

Heinemann is a registered trademark of
Harcourt Education Limited

© Harcourt Education, 2005

Copyright notice
All rights reserved. No part of this publication may be reproduced in any material form (including photocopying
or storing it in any medium by electronic means and whether or not transiently or incidentally to some other
use of this publication) without the prior written permission of the copyright owner, except in accordance with
the provisions of the Copyright, Designs and Patents Act 1988 or under the terms of a licence issued by the
Copyright Licensing Agency Ltd, 90 Tottenham Court Road, London W1T 4LP. Applications for the copyright
owner's written permission to reproduce any part of this publication should be addressed to the publisher.

First published 2005

10-digit ISBN: 0 435413 43 0
13-digit ISBN: 978 0 435413 43 9
09 08 07 06
10 9 8 7 6 5 4

Designed by Wild Apple Design
Produced by Kamae Design

Printed and bound in China by CTPS

Index compiled by Ian D Crane

Illustrated by John Storey, Geoff Ward and Kamae

CROYDON LIBRARIES	
021739341	
Bertrams	24.11.07
664 WOO	£13.50
LN1	FOO

Photographic acknowledgements
The authors and publisher should like to thank the following for permission to reproduce photographs:
Arnos Design Ltd, pp.80, 81 (all), 82 (all), 84 (all); Asda/Walmart, p.18; CCRFRA (Campden and Chorleywood
Food Research Association) p.13; Corbis, p.70; Getty Images/Food+E3pix, p.58 (top left); Harcourt Education/
Gareth Boden, pp.30, 100 (right), 102; Harcourt Education/Haddon Davies, pp.33, 73; Harcourt Education/Roger
Scruton, pp.62, 90 (left column); Harcourt Education/Tudor Photography, pp.12, 34, 35, 45 (bottom), 71, 73
(both), 75, 77, 90 (bottom left), 95, 98, 99 (all), 103, 104, 110, 111, 113, 114, 115, 117(left column), 122, 123
(right column); Harcourt Ltd, pp.31, 76, 94, 100(left); Heathcotes, p.121 (bottom); Lesley Woods pp.58 (A, B, C
& D), 59 (all), 120; New Covent Garden Food Company p.119 (all); Northcote Manor, p.121 (top); Pam Services,
p.45 (top); Photolibrary.com/food pix p.90 (top right); Popperfoto, p.74; Rex Features, pp.46, 123; Sainsbury's
p.115; The Anthony Blake Picture Library, p.91; United Biscuits pp.60 (both), 61(all), 78; Vegetarian Society
p.117.

Cover photograph by Science Photo Library
Cover Design by Wooden Ark

Picture research by Helen Reilly and Natalie Gray

The publisher would like to thank the following for permission to reproduce copyright material:

The British Nutrition Foundation for the poster on p.14; Fairtrade UK for the Fairtrade mark on p.34; Columbus
Eggs for the diagram on p.35; Chrysalis Books Group for the recipe page on p.43; Country Cakes for the images
and information on pp. 58-9; United Biscuits for the images and information on pp.60-61; Cauldron Foods
for the images and information on pp.80-85; Crown copyright material is reproduced with permissions of the
Controller of Her Majesty's Office, p.112; the gluten-free symbol on p.115 is reproduced with kind permission of
Sainsbury's Supermarkets Ltd; the vegetarian Society for the trademark on p.117.
AQA examination questions are reproduced by kind permission of the Assessment and Qualifications Alliance.
Please note that some of the questions used are NOT from the live examinations for the current specification.
New specifications for all GCSE subjects other than English and English Literature were introduced in 2003.

A special thanks to the students who allowed their coursework to be reproduced in this publication. Also, to the
people at Country Cakes and Cauldron Foods for their help in producing the case studies.

The publishers have made every effort to trace copyright holders. However, if any material has been incorrectly
acknowledged, we would be please to correct this at the earliest opportunity.

Contents

This book has been written to meet the requirements of the full and short course AQA specifications for GCSE Food Technology. The AQA specification is designed to meet the National Curriculum Orders and GCSE Subject Criteria for Design and Technology.

The programme of study for Design and Technology at Key Stage 4 requires you to develop your Design and Technology capability by applying knowledge and understanding of food technology when developing ideas, planning, making products and evaluating them.

AQA specification

The specification provides opportunities for you to develop Design and Technology capability throughout your course. It requires you to combine skills with knowledge and understanding in order to design and make quality products in quantity. It also provides opportunities for you to acquire and apply knowledge, skills and understanding through:

★ analysing and evaluating existing products and industrial processes
★ undertaking focused practical tasks to develop and demonstrate techniques
★ working out how to develop ideas, and plan and produce products
★ considering how past and present design and technology affects society
★ recognising the moral, cultural and environmental issues in design and technology situations
★ using ICT.

How will you be assessed?

You will be assessed in two ways. You will complete a coursework project making up 60% of your GCSE mark. You will also complete a 2-hour (1-hour for the short course) written exam at the end of the course that will make up 40% of your GCSE mark. In both the coursework and the written exam, you will be assessed on how you demonstrate your knowledge, skills and understanding in three ways:

★ of materials, components, processes, techniques and industrial practice (20%)
★ when designing and making quality products in quantity (60%)
★ when evaluating processes and products and examining the wider effects of design and technology on society (20%).

Most of your marks (60%) will be awarded for designing and making. Most of your designing and making will be completed in your coursework project.

How to use this book

This book will help you:

★ develop your food technology skills
★ develop your knowledge and understanding of food technology, specifically for the content requirements of the AQA specification
★ understand what is required for internal assessment (coursework) and how to get the best grades
★ prepare and revise for the written exam and understand how to get the best grades
★ develop key skills of communication, application of number, information and communications technology, working with others, problem solving and improving your own learning through your food technology work.

This book is divided into the following parts:

★ Part 1 What you need to know: this is the main part of the book and contains sections 1–6
★ Part 2 Doing your coursework project: this contains section 7 and gives advice on how to plan and produce your coursework, helping you get the best marks possible
★ Part 3 Preparing for the exam: this comprises section 8 and gives advice on what examiners are looking for, how to prepare for the exam and how to get the best marks you can.

This book is written in double-page chapters. Each chapter includes:

★ specification links to show which modules of the AQA specification are covered by the chapter
★ an introduction showing what you will learn from the chapter
★ activities that reinforce and develop learning
★ a summary of the chapter to help with revision.

Chapters that include an activity involving the use of ICT are identified by the ICT icon **ICT** at the top of the page.

AQA Food Technology 10.5 and 10.6

Numbering is used on each double-paged chapter to show which section of the AQA Food Technology specification the chapter matches.

ICT D1 Some chapters of Part One are also useful for the coursework project. This is identified by showing the relevant coursework assessment criteria at the top of the chapter. Here, 'D' refers to Designing and 'M' refers to Making. Along with the numbering, these are taken from the coursework project assessment criteria given in section 16.3 of the AQA specification. Please note that grades F and G have fewer assessment criteria, so the numbering here is based on grades A-E for consistency.

Some chapters might also include:

★ coursework boxes: these show how particular chapters in Part 1 are relevant to your coursework, so you should keep this information in mind when completing your project. You will also need to make sure you read Part 2 so that you understand exactly what you need to do for your project

★ case studies: these give real examples of how the processes and knowledge you are learning are applied in real life.

At the end of each section there are relevant examples of exam questions and the marks available. These will help you practise and revise for the exam.

Finally, there is also a glossary at the end of the book to explain words identified in bold text. This will be useful as you are going through your course and also when you come to revise for the exam or do your coursework.

Websites

There are links to relevant web sites in this book. In order to ensure that the links are up-to-date, that the links work, and that the sites aren't inadvertently linked to sites that could be considered offensive, we have made the links available on the Heinemann website at www.heinemann.co.uk/hotlinks. When you access the site, the express code is 3430P.

Short course

If you are following the short course, you will need to use just some of the chapters in this book. You will need guidance from your teacher on how to use this book and which chapters to use.

1 Research

This section covers the sensory function of ingredients and products, and looks at the different research and evaluation techniques you need to carry out during your course. Sensory evaluation is a key skill to learn and use during this course.

What's in this section?

Evaluating an individual product

In this chapter you will:

★ learn how to evaluate an individual food product for a specific **target group** or need.

Product analysis is part of the research you should carry out so that you can design and make quality food products. To analyse something means to examine a product in detail. If you are thinking of making a certain product and want to find out more about it, you need to look at a selection of similar existing products. If you want to find out more about cakes, you need to analyse a number of cakes. To do this, you need to:

- disassemble the cake (take it to pieces)
- use **sensory evaluation**
- look at the information on the packaging
- examine the packaging materials.

Product analysis is not just eating food

Disassembling the cake

To analyse a product, you can use either physical or imaginary disassembly. Disassembly is the process of taking something apart and looking at the individual parts.

Physical disassembly

A cup cake would be easy to disassemble physically by taking the icing off. You could then weigh the icing and the cake separately. This is a good thing to do to understand all the different proportions of ingredients. Another example of a physical disassembly could be a sausage roll. You can work out the percentage of meat to pastry.

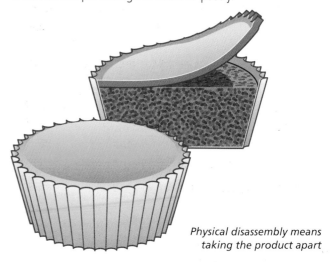

Physical disassembly means taking the product apart

Imaginary disassembly

An imaginary disassemble is when you look at a product and try to work out what is in it. This is suitable for a product that might be difficult to physically disassemble, for example one with a sauce such as a curry. You might look at a small proportion of the curry to identify some of its ingredients. You could draw it to keep a record of what it looked like. You could also use the list of ingredients on the label to help you with this task, which shows what the manufacturer used to make the dish. You can also get other information from the label, for example:

- a description of the product, often using adjectives to persuade you to buy it
- a picture of the dish
- information on how to store and prepare it
- the 'best before' date
- details about the manufacturer and where to send any complaints
- the quantity in the packet
- the food's nutritional content
- any special advice such as suitable for vegetarians
- what materials are used for the packaging and why.

Sensory evaluation

Sensory evaluation or analysis is a way of describing the characteristics of a product using all the senses.

To do a sensory evaluation of a cupcake, you would write down up to eight **sensory descriptors** – words that could be used to describe it such as crumbly, moist or sweet. The words should reflect all the senses: sight, smell, taste, touch and hearing (think of the crunch when eating a juicy apple, for example). These words are called product attributes. They should allow someone who cannot see or taste the product to know exactly what it is like.

As you taste the cake, write down a score of between 1 to 5 against each of the attributes, where 1 is poor and 5 is very good. These scores can be converted into an **attribute profile** using a spreadsheet program on a computer.

As you can see, this attribute profile shows that the person thought the cake was very sweet and needed a little more chocolate in it. They thought the texture and mouth feel (soft, crumbly) was good and the appearance (colour, smooth icing) was rated highly.

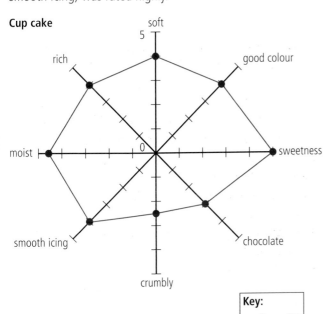

Cup cake

An attribute profile for a cupcake

Packaging

A product evaluation should also consider the packaging itself. Ask yourself questions such as: what materials are used and why? What are their properties? Are there any disadvantages to using any of these materials? What is the environmental impact of this packaging? Is too much packaging being used? What does the packaging tell you about the product?

Evaluating packaging is important. You will have to think about how the product you want to design will be manufactured and packaged.

[ic] Coursework

Product evaluations help you to develop your outline **specification**.

✎ Activities

1 Evaluate a food product of your choice. You should include a disassembly, a sensory evaluation and an evaluation of the labelling and packaging. Choose from:
   - a cherry bakewell tart
   - a cornish pasty
   - a pizza
   - a samosa
   - a fondant fancy
   - a mince pie.

2 Use a spreadsheet program to draw an attribute profile for your product. What do you notice? How will this help you when you design a similar product?

Summary

★ Product evaluation involves disassembly, sensory evaluation, and labelling and packaging evaluation.

★ Product evaluation is important because it helps you to decide what you want your product to be like.

Research

In this chapter you will:

★ learn how to compare food products in a systematic way

★ learn how comparative evaluation is used in the food manufacturing industry.

To evaluate something means to think about the quality of that product and how good it is. A comparative evaluation is when two or more products are evaluated against the same points. Looking at more than one product will provide you with more information about existing products than if you looked at just one product.

Five students have each brought a different packet of biscuits to the lesson. They are going to do a comparative evaluation. They will compare similar products to help them decide how they would like their product to be.

A comparative product evaluation

They start by comparing the price and the number of biscuits in each packet. They also read the labels and look at the packaging. Then they weigh and measure one biscuit from each packet and make a note of the colour. They simulate a testing booth (a separate area away from any distractions including noise and light) and put the biscuits first on a coloured background, then on a white background to see the colour change. They record all their findings in a table like the one below.

Finally, the students get to taste the biscuits, making sure they cleanse their palates by having a drink of water between tasting each biscuit. For this comparison evaluation, they use ranking and rating tests. They rate each type of biscuit according to how sweet they think it is and how crunchy it is. Then they rank the biscuits in order of preference.

At the end of this **sensory evaluation**, the students have a clear idea of how sweet or crunchy they like a biscuit to be and which flavours they prefer.

Comparisons in the food industry

This kind of product evaluation is carried out all the time in the food manufacturing industry for different reasons. In a large company there are tasting sessions every day in the **quality control** department to make sure the products produced stay at the same quality.

Most large food manufacturers have product development departments. They carry out tasting sessions when they want to develop a new product or improve an existing one.

Type of biscuit	Price (£)	Number in packet	Weight of biscuit (g)	Size of biscuit (mm)	Colour of biscuit	Packaging details	Rank in order of sweetness	Rank in order of crunchiness	Rank in order of preference
Value Choc Chip	0.59	45					1		
Slimmers' Rich Tea	0.89	25					4		
Apple and Cinnamon Thins	1.29	15					2		
Party Rings	0.99	12					5		
Coconut and Raisin	0.89	18					3		

Use a table to record your findings when doing a comparative product evaluation

The group below are taking part in a tasting session to evaluate vegetable lasagnes made by their competitors so that they have a 'benchmark' or guideline for the kind of vegetable lasagne they want to produce. They collated their results and produced an **attribute profile**. The tasters also wrote notes giving a more detailed description of what they wanted their lasagne to be like:

'A good quantity of sliced mushrooms, a small amount of aubergine, small pieces of onion, some diced tomatoes, more garlic flavour than herbs, and quite a rich tomato flavour. Not too much pasta and more vegetables than white sauce. Some grated cheese on the top.'

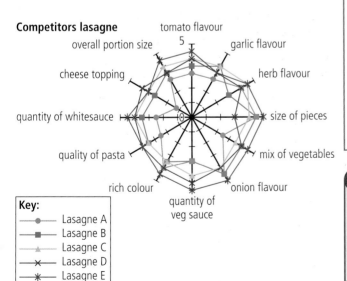

A tasting session

Competitors lasagne

Key:
— ● — Lasagne A
— ■ — Lasagne B
— ▲ — Lasagne C
— ✕ — Lasagne D
— ✳ — Lasagne E

The tasters' attribute profile. Lasagne E got the highest results, so this lasagne will be used as the company's benchmark when they start to plan the recipe for their own lasagne

Coursework

Comparison evaluations will help you to decide on your outline **specification**. This is a list of what your product should be like.

Activity

Write a profile of what you think your ideal pizza would be like, then carry out your own comparison product evaluation of three or four different pizzas. Create an attribute profile to compare the pizzas you have sampled.

Pizza	Appearance	Taste	Texture	Smell	Total
1	3	4	3	3	13
2	4	3	2	3	12
3	3	3			
4					

Comments:
_____
_____
_____
_____
_____

Key:
5 Excellent
4 Very Good
3 Good
2 Satisfactory
1 Just satisfactory
X Unacceptable

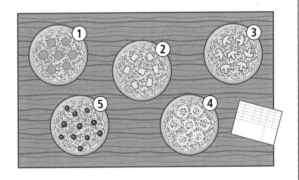

Summary

★ Comparison evaluation compares a range of similar products. They can help to rank **consumer** (customer) preferences and also identify what an 'ideal' product would be like.

Research

Sensory analysis

In this chapter you will learn:
★ how sensory analysis can help to develop quality food products.

The senses

You use your five sensory organs (ears, nose, tongue, skin and ears) when you eat. These give information about the food you are eating. For example:

- you hear if fizzy drinks are fresh
- you smell food such as fish and chips
- you see attractive or unattractive food like snails
- you taste food, especially things like lemons and jelly beans
- you touch food like a crusty bread roll and a ripe peach.

If you were blindfolded and held your nose while you drank blackcurrant cordial, you might not know what the flavour was. Try it! If you were given some orange jelly to eat, you would be surprised if it did not taste of oranges. If someone broke a biscuit in half with a 'snap', you would expect the biscuit to be crunchy and crisp, not soft and chewy. If, at the school canteen, there were two plates of cottage pie like the ones in the photo, you would probably choose the one on the right because it 'looks the nicest'. If you were given some sour-smelling milk to make scones, you might say, 'I can't use that – it's "off".' In fact, sour milk makes a better-tasting scone!

Which plate would you choose?

Sensory analysis

The characteristics of food that affect our sensory organs are called **organoleptic properties**. Sensory analysis means tasting food to work out what these qualities are. It is carried out because it helps to answer questions about food products in three main areas:

- description: what does the product taste like? How does a change in production, storage and packaging affect its taste?
- discrimination: is the product different or similar to a competitor's product or a low-fat product? Would people notice the difference?
- preference: how much do people like the product? Which parts do they like? Is the product an improvement to a previous one?

Smell is just one of five sensory organs that give us information about food

Case Study

Sensory analysis in manufacturing

Food manufacturers use sensory analysis to develop new products and check the quality of existing ones. It can be used to:

- monitor **prototypes** (trialled ideas), checking that the **specification** (what a product should be like) or improvements are being met
- check whether a new product is likely to be acceptable to, or popular with, **consumers**
- demonstrate new products to a **marketing** or sales team
- find out whether people can distinguish between different products, for example low-fat products compared with traditional products
- measure **shelf life** by testing samples at different times after production to see how eating quality is affected
- carry out **quality control**, regularly monitoring samples from the production line against the original specification
- describe specific characteristics about a product, for example sweetness.

Food testing booths like these help to maintain a controlled environment for sensory analysis

Test your knowledge

Describe the senses you use when eating:

- **a** freshly baked bread
- **b** a red apple
- **c** garlic mushrooms
- **d** a jam doughnut.

A controlled environment for sensory analysis

To obtain reliable results from sensory analysis during a product evaluation or after a product has been made, you need to make sure the people tasting are not distracted or influenced in any way.

- Provide individual booths, free from cooking smells and with controlled lighting.
- Samples of one product should be the same size, served on identical white dishes at the correct temperature. If more than one sample is being tasted and compared, they should be coded.
- Water (or lime juice) and crackers should be consumed between samples to clear the mouth.
- There should be clear instructions for the tester with a straightforward response sheet to record their results.

Activity

Make a blue jelly using gelatine, sugar and blue food colouring. Divide the jelly equally into three bowls. Flavour the three jellies with peppermint, orange and strawberry essence. When the jellies have set, carry out a fair test in a controlled environment to find out peoples' comments and preferences.

Summary

★ Sensory analysis is the process of systematically tasting foods and recording the experiences of the taster.

★ Sensory analysis is a key activity in food technology as it guides decisions about food products.

Research

In this chapter you will:
★ learn how to use **sensory tests**
★ learn how to choose the right test for the right purpose so that you can find out people's views and preferences of products.

Different tests are used in sensory analysis to obtain different kinds of information. The three main techniques used are descriptive, preference and discrimination tests.

Descriptive tests

The most versatile test to use in school is the descriptive test (sometimes called attribute testing or star profiles/diagrams). This test can be used at every stage of developing a food product. It can be used to:
- evaluate existing products
- decide on the sensory characteristics of a product to be made (part of a **specification**)
- evaluate a product you have made against certain sensory characteristics
- compare similarities or differences in products you have made or in existing products.

A wide range of vocabulary is used to describe the sensory characteristics of food products. Each sense uses different descriptive words.

Using descriptive tests to evaluate against specifications

Opposite is an **attribute profile** created by someone who has made a vegetable quiche. The product specification says it should have buttery, crisp and crumbly pastry, with a soft, creamy and cheesy filling with crunchy and colourful vegetables included in it.

It is easy to tell from the attribute profile how to make changes to improve the product. This is because attribute profile diagrams are visual. They are an easy way to show which characteristics are popular and which are not. The pastry is almost perfect so does not need changing. The filling needs to include more cream and a little more cheese. A lot more colourful vegetables need to be added but they still need to be crunchy.

Descriptive tests are subjective tests. This means they supply information about people's likes and dislikes of a product. Subjective tests are all about people's personal opinions, and people have different opinions.

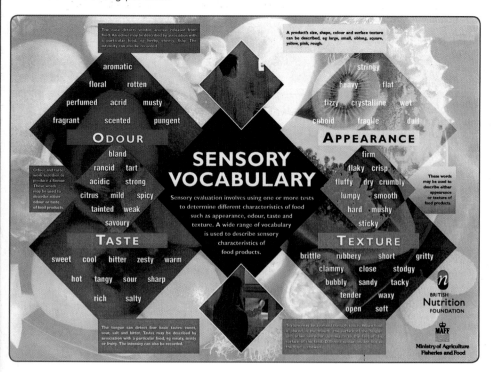

Sensory characteristics can be described using many words. This poster, from the British Nutrition Foundation, provides a wide vocabulary of words that can be used when describing food.

Vegetable quiche

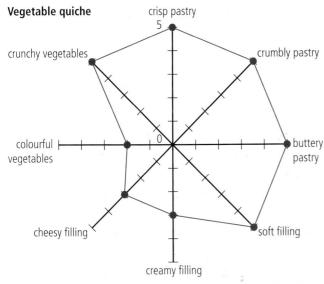

An attribute profile for a vegetable quiche

Preference tests

Preference tests are also subjective. There are three kinds of preference tests:

- paired comparison test: this is when tasters are asked to state which of two samples they prefer, for example pastry made with margarine or butter
- ranking test: this is when tasters are asked to rank, in order of preference, a range of similar food products, for example a spaghetti bolognese sauce with different amounts of tomato purée or herbs added
- hedonic ranking test: this shows how much testers like or dislike a product. Products are scored on a scale of 5 or 9 points.

Rating Score	1 like extremely	2 like a little	3 neither like nor dislike	4 dislike a little	5 dislike a lot
	😀	🙂	😐	🙁	☹️
sample △					
sample ▢					
sample ◯					

Hedonic ranking tests show how much people like or dislike a product

Discrimination tests

Unlike descriptive and preference tests, discrimination tests are objective tests. Their aim is to evaluate specific characteristics such as sweetness or crumbliness – see the table below for an example. They show the quality of particular tastes or textures, not opinions. There are five kinds of discrimination tests. The two most commonly used are:

- ranking test: tasters rank samples in order of a specific characteristic such as sweetness in a biscuit or flakiness in pastry
- scoring tests using scales: samples are scored on different scales to evaluate a particular characteristic such as how crumbly different pastries are.

Biscuit	Very crumbly	Crumbly	Slightly crumbly	Not very crumbly	Not crumbly at all
1					
2					
3					

Activities

1 Make three samples of shortcrust pastry using different kinds of fat and mixtures of fat such as margarine and lard. Use preference tests to find out the most suitable fat to use.

2 Make four samples of biscuit using different quantities of sugar in each. Use discrimination tests to find out which biscuit tastes the sweetest and whether tasters can identify the differences in sugar content.

Summary

★ There are descriptive, preference and discrimination tests.

★ Each test is suitable for different purposes and situations.

★ Descriptive tests are easy to use if evaluating food products against a specification.

★ Tests have to be fair to get accurate results.

Writing a questionnaire

In this chapter you will:
- ★ learn how to write an effective questionnaire
- ★ learn how to collate and analyse the results.

Product analysis involves your opinions and those of a few more people. You may find it helpful to find out the views of even more people. This means that when you produce your food product, you will have considered a broader range of opinions and people are more likely to buy it.

The way to get these opinions is to carry out a survey. A survey is a way of gathering opinions from a range of people on a particular subject. To do this, you need to produce a questionnaire and ask as broad a range of people as possible. However, you have to ask the right people the right questions.

Let's look at two imaginary companies to see how to complete a successful survey. Mr David Knowittal and Mr Ian Carefulle have both set up companies that are going to produce sandwiches for small outlets. Mr Knowittal quickly

puts together six questions and asks ten friends for their views. Below is a summary of the answers he received.

Questions 3, 5 and 6 are open questions – this means they allow people to give any answer they want and sometimes the answers are vague. It is difficult to analyse the answers to open questions.

Mr Carefulle worked out exactly what he wanted to learn from his questionnaire. This made it easy for him to write relevant questions. He asked a selection of people coming out of a sandwich shop. Opposite is a summary of their replies.

The questions in Mr Carefulle's survey are closed questions. These questions give a choice of answers, making the results easier to collate, present and analyse.

Using graphs and charts

Using visual forms of communication such as graphs and charts makes it easier to present, interpret and understand questionnaire results. You can use a spreadsheet program like Microsoft Excel to help you.

Questionnaires are not used just for ideas; they are also part of the evaluation process. Mr Carefulle knows what people like, and once he has started to make sandwiches he could ask his customers what they think of them so he can continue to improve his service.

Mr Knowittal and Mr Carefulle work on their questionnaires

Coursework

Questionnaires help you to decide on design criteria **specification** points (what a product or products should be like) and generally assist with the evaluation process while designing and making.

1 Do you like sandwiches? Yes 9   No 1 — Difficult to count so many

2 Which do you prefer; brown or white bread? White 6   Brown 4

3 What fillings do you like? 30 different fillings were given — What type? What about mayonnaise?

4 Do you like salad cream in your sandwiches? Yes 6   No 4

5 How much would you pay for a sandwich? The prices ranged from 99p to £2.50

6 How often do you eat a sandwich for lunch? Most answered usually every day — But they could have made it themselves!

Mr Knowittal's questionnaire

It is useful to know what else, apart from sandwiches, are bought

Do you like sandwiches?

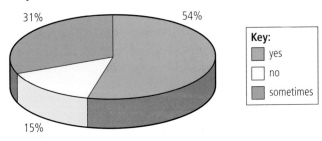

31%   54%

Key:
- yes
- no
- sometimes

15%

1 What do you prefer to eat for your lunch?

Sandwich made with sliced bread	6
Bagel	5
Pasty, pie or sausage roll	3
Salad	3
Soup	1
Other	2

2 What kind of bread do you like your sandwich to be made of?

White sliced bread	5
Brown sliced bread	4
Malted bread	3
Bagette	2
Ciabatta	1
Tortilla wrap	2
Flavoured bread (e.g. tomato)	4

Very specific questions – you can count the answers

What kind of bread do you like?

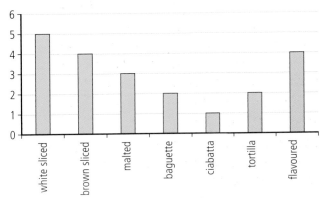

Pie charts and bar charts are helpful ways of showing your results

3 Which ingredients do you like as sandwich fillings?

Cheese 10	Ham 6	Chicken 4
Beef 5	Pork 1	Sausage 2
Bacon 4	Tomato 12	Lettuce 6
Cucumber 4	Sweetcorn 4	Onion 5
Pepper 3	Grated carrot 1	Tuna 5
Roast vegetables 3	Prawns 4	Salmon 3
Mayonnaise 7	Salad cream 3	

4 Which of these combinations do you prefer?

Cheese, ham and tomato	12
Roast vegetables and brie cheese	4
Beef, cooked onions and tomatoes	8
Tuna, sweetcorn, lettuce and mayonnaise	7

5 How much would you pay for a sandwich?

No more than £1.50	3
No more than £1.99	7
No more than £2.25	12
No more than £2.50	5
No more than £2.75	2

A range of prices makes it easier to analyse the results

6 How often do you buy a sandwich from a shop in one week?

Every day	9
2 or 3 times a week	12
Once a week	5
Never	2

Focus on the information you actually want

Mr Carefulle's questionnaire

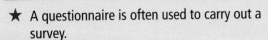
Activities

1 Write a short questionnaire for a food product you want to design and make. Use appropriate closed questions. Think about who the product is aimed at and where it will be sold. You could also consider what ingredients it will include and the size of your product.

2 Present your results in graph form using a spreadsheet program such as Microsoft Excel.

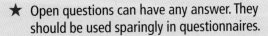
Summary

★ A questionnaire is often used to carry out a survey.

★ Open questions can have any answer. They should be used sparingly in questionnaires.

★ Closed questions provide a range of possible answers. It is easier to analyse the response to closed questions.

> **In this chapter you will:**
> ★ learn how to find out about existing products to help you to think about the kind of products you could design and to help generate ideas.

The Internet is a useful tool. It can be used to chat to friends, to buy things and for research. It is useful in food technology as an easy way to look at the wide range of existing food products rather than just a few that are used in product evaluations.

Using supermarket websites

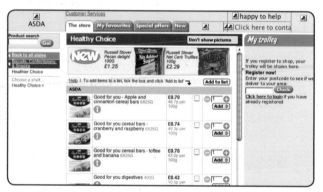

Supermarket websites are useful for looking at existing products

Supermarket websites are a useful source of information. On many of these sites you can browse through the shelves without having to register as a customer and look at the wide range of products available including the selling price. There are two ways to record and present the information you need in a compact way. Looking at biscuits, for example:

1 Create an information chart like the one below, showing the range of biscuits available together with the packet weight and price. Include comments about the biscuits.
2 Copy and paste packaging images into a desktop publishing file like the one on the next page. Include information about the packet weight and price together with some comments.

Internet alternatives

If access to the Internet is difficult, you could visit supermarkets or shops to see what ranges are available. By visiting a variety of different shops, you can obtain information about a wide range of products. You should record your findings in a chart or table like the one below.

Sketching existing products

Sometimes it is relevant to sketch the products available. For example, when you are looking at specialist bread

Type of biscuit	Weight (g)	Price (£)	Comments
Choc chip	300	0.66	A basic cookie – a bit boring
Double choc chip	100	0.54	Looks full of chocolate chips
Triple choc chip	450	0.98	Dark colour with two types of chips – too rich
Smartprice choc chip	200	0.27	Not many chocolate chips
Ginger nuts	300	0.45	Colourful
Malted milk	200	0.38	A nice decoration on the top and rectangular shape
Coconut rings	300	0.48	A ring shape is a good idea
Custard creams	300	0.44	Chunky and probably sweet
Fig rolls	200	0.42	Looks juicy
Garibaldi	200	0.56	Thin, but looks interesting
Black treacle creams	200	0.60	A dark custard cream

An information chart using internet research or shop visits

products that are shaped and decorated in different ways, you could make simple sketches of each product. This will help you start to think about different shapes and sizes you could create.

Biscuits

These were new in shops in Winter 2003. they were an immediate hit and were quite cheap as well. Reviews were usually very good.

These are 'Ginger Crunch Creams and are also quite new biscuits with a new Fox's logo. They have been have been described as 'good old delicious ginger biscuits though sandwiched with a smooth creamy filling'.

This is the 'Rocky Rounds' biscuits and are in standard Rocky packaging (red and yellow) . In this case the biscuits are mini dome shaped bite sizes biscuits. They are priced at around £4.

These are Moores Dorset Biscuits and are made only in Dorset. They are available to order from the website and reviews are usually very good

This is one of the classic chocolate Bourbon biscuits that have been around for a long time and are one of the countries favourite biscuits. They are bought in packets not individually and most people think they taste very sweet and tasty.

This example of a student's completed sheet shows how to present information in a desktop publishing program

If you go to the information desk and explain the purpose of your visit you will not end up like this!

Other uses of the Internet

The Internet can also be used as a search tool to generate ideas. For example, you could use a search engine to find recipes for your food product.

- Give yourself a time limit, say a maximum of one hour.
- Carefully choose the words to be searched to narrow your results. For example, the words 'prawn toast' give 5000 results, but searching on 'sesame prawn toast' gives just 237 results.
- Read each recipe through first to make sure you understand the ingredients and how to make it. Recipes from other countries use different measurements and names for some ingredients, so you may find it helpful to search UK websites only.
- Decide exactly how many recipes you need and make sure you print off only a small selection.
- Remember to use the Internet sensibly.

Another way to use the Internet is to find out more about a particular topic or product. For example, you could use a search engine again to find information about folic acid or special diets.

Coursework

It is important to remember not to just print the information from the screen – your research must be concise and relevant. Looking at a wide range of products is a useful piece of research, and looking at recipes will help you to come up with ideas.

Activity

Use the Internet to find out about fresh vegetable soups available from two supermarkets. You need to provide information on the types of soup, weight, price and comments. Allow yourself a time limit of one hour to obtain the information, then use a blank version of the table opposite to present your data.

Summary

★ The Internet is a useful tool for research of existing products and other areas too.

Research

Exam questions

1 A food manufacturer wants to develop a new range of sweet baked products.

Products already on sale

a The design team buys and compares similar products. Give three reasons why this is done. *(6 marks)*

b Name two methods used to find out which baked products the consumer would like to buy. *(2 marks)*
(AQA/NEAB 1999)

2 a Name two methods of collecting information to find out which multicultural products consumers would like to buy. *(2 marks)*

b How could the results of information collected help a manufacturer to develop food products? *(3 marks)*
(AQA/NEAB 2000)

3 A manufacturer is asked to design a range of hand-held snack food products for sale in the supermarket. Explain how the following research methods can be useful when designing new products.

a The study of existing products already on the market. *(3 marks)*

b A questionnaire given to supermarket customers. *(3 marks)*
(AQA/NEAB 2001)

4 Describe ways in which a manufacturer may use a computer to obtain information about barbecue products. *(4 marks)*
(AQA 2003)

5 A sauce manufacturer has asked the test kitchen to produce a smooth, spicy, tomato sauce. A sensory analysis of the product gave the following results:

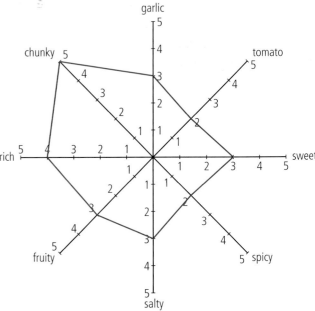

From the information given in the star profile sensory analysis:

a identify two areas for improvement. *(2 marks)*

b How could the test kitchen use this information in the development of a smooth, spicy tomato sauce? *(4 marks)*
(AQA/NEAB 2000)

2 The function of ingredients

This section looks at the function of ingredients used in food products.

The nutritional and physical functions of ingredients are studied, as well as extra functions some ingredients have. Understanding of the function of ingredients enables you to develop food products successfully. Practical experience of the function of ingredients is important.

What's in this section?

2.1 Nutritional functions of carbohydrates

> In this chapter you will:
> ★ learn about the need for a balanced **diet**.
> ★ learn about carbohydrates, one of the macronutrients.

A balanced diet

You need food to keep you alive, but some foods are better for us than others. There are no 'good' or 'bad' foods; healthy eating is all about getting the balance right. You need to be aware of the balance of healthy eating.

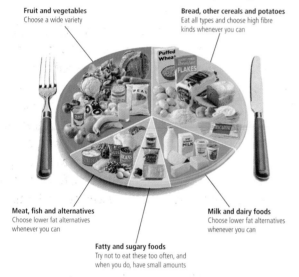

Fruit and vegetables
Choose a wide variety

Bread, other cereals and potatoes
Eat all types and choose high fibre kinds whenever you can

Meat, fish and alternatives
Choose lower fat alternatives whenever you can

Milk and dairy foods
Choose lower fat alternatives whenever you can

Fatty and sugary foods
Try not to eat these too often, and when you do, have small amounts

Eating healthily is all about balance

The balance of good health is based on the government's eight guidelines for a healthy diet. The key message is that a balance of foods should be eaten to achieve a healthy diet. This balance should be achieved over a week or two, not from just one meal.

The government has also published recommendations to make sure everyone gets enough of each nutrient to meet their needs. The table above shows the daily recommendations. At the moment, on average, people are eating too much fat, sugar and salt, and not enough NSP (fibre) and starch. If you understand what nutrients are, what these nutrients do and where you can find them, you can make sure you produce nutritionally balanced food products. It is important to encourage people to eat a balanced diet by making nutritionally balanced products.

Nutrient	Dietary recommendations per day
Energy value of food	Varies with age, gender and activity, but average: 2550 kcal for adult male 1940 kcal for adult female
Protein	55g for adult male 45g for adult female
Fat	No more than 35% of energy value
Carbohydrates of which starch	50% of energy value 39% of energy value
Sugars (non-milk extrinsic sugars – NME)	11% of energy value
NSP (dietary fibre)	18g for adults
Vitamins	Based on individual needs
Minerals	Based on individual needs

Daily recommendations for a healthy diet

Nutrients

A nutrient is part of a food that does a particular job in the body. Nearly all foods contain more than one nutrient. There are **macronutrients** (needed in large quantities, such as carbohydrates, fat and protein), **micronutrients** (needed in small quantities) and non-nutrients (water and NSP) that are all needed by the body to stay alive.

Carbohydrates

Carbohydrates are one of the most common and important macronutrients and are found in most baked products. They are used for energy, but if too much is eaten, the body stores the extra as fat – it is often carbohydrates, not fats, that make people fat. There are three types of carbohydrates: sugar, starch and NSP.

Sugar

Sugar is a mono or disaccharide, which means it is a simple sugar that is easily digested to make glucose, required by blood for energy. Too many sugary foods makes the blood sugar levels rise and fall because of rushes of glucose to the blood. Sugar also rots the teeth because it combines easily with the bacteria in the mouth to produce acids that attack and damage tooth enamel.

Sugary foods often contain only other macronutrients, not the micronutrients needed by the body (see Chapter 2.3). Current recommendations are that we should cut down the amount of sugar we eat to 11% of our energy intake.

Starch

Starch is a polysaccharide, which means it is a complex sugar. It needs to be broken down by digestion before the energy can be used. As it is a slow energy releaser, the body's blood sugar levels stay fairly level and there is a gentle release of glucose to the blood. Starchy foods contain the micronutrients needed by the body, so they are a balanced nutrient.

Foods containing large amounts of starch incude cereals such as wheat (flour, pasta and bread), rice, maize (corn) and root vegetables such as potatoes and yams. Other root vegetables contain some starch. Fruits contain less starch, but bananas are an exception. We should be increasing the amount of starch we eat to 39% of our energy intake.

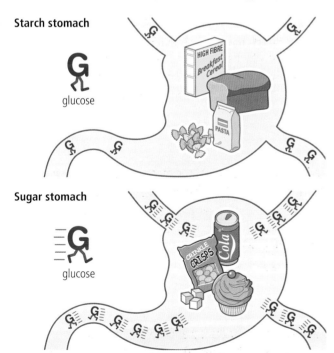

Eating sugar results in a rush of glucose into the blood. Eating starch results in a slower release of glucose into the blood.

NSP (dietary fibre)

NSP is a non-starch polysaccharide and is not a nutrient in the same way as starch and sugar because it does not provide energy. It cannot be digested by the human body but it does aid many digestive processes. The simple explanation of how it works is to say that it 'keeps you regular' or that it prevents constipation! It makes waste products bulkier and lighter so that they easily work their way through the body.

It has been suggested that NSP also helps prevent certain cancers and other diseases such as appendicitis and haemorrhoids (piles). High-fibre foods are also filling, so can help to control body weight.

There are two types of NSP, soluble and insoluble. Soluble NSP becomes sticky when combined with water. It feeds intestinal bacteria and because of this it is linked to low cholesterol levels. Examples include oats, rice, barley and fruit. Insoluble NSP acts as a sponge as it passes through the body. It soaks up water and increases the bulk of stools. Examples include wheat, pulses (beans, peas, lentils) and the skin of many fruit and vegetables. The important thing is to ensure that enough NSP is eaten overall. Foods high in fibre are wholegrain cereals such as wheat, rice and oats, and fruit and vegetables.

Activities

1 Complete a making activity to improve the fibre content of biscuits by using a variety of soluble and insoluble fibre sources such as wholemeal flour, brown flour, porridge oats and oatmeal. Are the taste and texture acceptable?

2 Model small quantities of biscuits using different quantities of sugar. Use a preference test to find out which quantity produces an acceptable sweetness.

Summary

★ It is important to produce food products that fit into the balance of good health.

★ Carbohydrates are used for energy. It is better to eat starchy foods rather than sugary foods.

★ Fibre is a non-nutrient that aids digestion.

2.2 Nutritional functions of fat and protein

> **In this chapter you will:**
> ★ learn about fat and protein, both macronutrients.

Macronutrients are needed in large quantities by the body for energy and growth.

Fat

Fat is a macronutrient that is used for energy. It is a concentrated way to obtain energy as, weight for weight, it provides just over twice as much as either carbohydrate or protein. This means that if you eat fatty foods, it is easy to get more energy than your body needs. Any extra energy is then stored in the body as fat.

You do need some fats as they provide fat-soluble vitamins A and D (some of the **micronutrients** the body needs). They also provide certain fatty acids such as Omega 3 and Omega 6, which are both essential to the structure and function of the body's cells. These fats are called 'essential' because they cannot be manufactured by the human body. We should be consuming Omega 3 and 6 in a ratio of 1:1. Most peoples' diets mean they are consuming them in a ratio of 1:20. Fat also surrounds and protects our vital organs such as our kidneys, and the fat under our skin helps keep us warm.

Examples of fats are butter, margarine, oil, lard and suet. Fat in food comes from animal sources (butter, lard and suet) or vegetable sources (margarine and oil). Fat is also 'hidden' in some meat products such as sausages and burgers, meaning you cannot see it.

The fats from animal sources are saturated fats that the liver makes into cholesterol. High blood cholesterol is a major risk factor in the development of heart disease. Fats from vegetable sources are poly or mono unsaturated.

Type of fat	Source
saturated	animal, butter, lard, fatty meat products
monounsaturated	olive oil, rapeseed oil, some nuts
polyunsaturated	margarine, sunflower oil

The different types of fat and their sources

These are thought to reduce the amount of cholesterol the liver produces. We should be aiming to reduce how much fat we eat so that it is only 35% of our energy intake.

Protein

Protein is needed for growth and repair of body tissue, muscles and blood cells. It comes from animal sources such as eggs, meat, fish, and dairy products such as cheese and yoghurt. Protein also comes from vegetable sources including beans, peas, lentils, nuts, seeds and cereals like rice and wheat (flour and pasta).

In the UK it is easy to get enough protein in our **diet** as we have enough money to buy these protein foods. However, often we eat more than our body needs. Excess protein is converted into glucose in the liver and used as energy.

Protein is broken down by the body into amino acids, which are then made into new proteins that our body needs. There are twenty amino acids that make up proteins. Our bodies can actually make eleven of them, but you must get the other nine from food. The special nine amino acids are called essential amino acids.

High and low biological value protein

All animal proteins contain the nine amino acids our bodies cannot make. This means our bodies can make use of this

Complementary meals: baked beans on toast and hummus on pitta bread

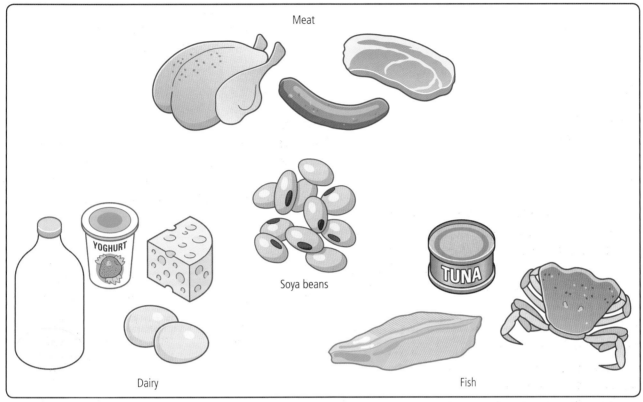

Meat

Soya beans

YOGHURT

TUNA

Dairy

Fish

These foods are all HBV (high biological value) proteins.

protein. These proteins are said to have a high biological value (HBV).

All except one of the vegetable proteins have at least one or more of these nine essential amino acids missing, which means that, if eaten on their own, the body cannot use the protein. These vegetable proteins are said to have a low biological value (LBV). So, if you eat a bowl of baked beans on their own, your body cannot use the protein in them. If the body is to use the vegetable protein, a mixture of vegetables must be eaten together to complement each other. Examples of complementary meals are beans on toast, hummus and pitta bread, chapatis and dhal, vegetarian chilli and rice. For example, the missing amino acids in the baked beans are found in the wheat that makes the toast. So, the body can now use the protein. This 'complementing' of vegetable proteins is important for people who eat no meat or dairy products, or for those who have reduced their intake of these foods.

Activities

1 Which protein-rich foods could be added to bread as extra ingredients to increase its protein content? Compare your answer with a partner.

2 Design a leaflet aimed at young children that explains why bread, which is full of starch, is better for you than cakes or biscuits, which contain lots of sugar and fat.

Summary

★ Fat is a compact energy provider. You need some fat in your diet, but it is easy to eat too much.

★ Some fats are thought to be better for you than others.

★ Proteins are present in many animal and vegetable foods.

★ Vegetable proteins need to be combined to provide the best nutritional value.

The function of ingredients

Nutritional functions of micronutrients

In this chapter you will:

★ learn about **micronutrients**

★ learn how and where micronutrients are used in food products.

Staying indoors all the time could lead to a deficiency of vitamin D

Micronutrients are needed by the body in smaller quantities than **macronutrients**. Sometimes micronutrients are forgotten when designing food products. But, even though they are only needed in small quantities, they are essential for health. It is easy to adapt food products to increase the amount of micronutrients in a product.

The information in the table below explains what these micronutrients are used for and which foods are good at providing them.

Minerals

Sodium

It is easy to eat too much salt (sodium chloride) because it is found in a lot of foods. Salt adds flavour to food and helps to preserve it. If you do not add salt to food such as bread, you need to add an alternative flavour like herbs or garlic, otherwise the bread will not taste good. Government advice says on average you should be eating no more than 6 grams of salt a day, of which no more than $2\frac{1}{2}$ grams should be sodium.

Micronutrient	Job in the body	Foods high in this nutrient
Sodium	Maintains the fluid balance in cells and helps with the correct function of nerve cells	Most processed foods
Calcium	Needed for teeth and bones, as well as blood clotting, muscle contraction and enzyme secretion	Cheese, yoghurt, cream and butter. Calcium is added to white flour and is also found in green leafy vegetables, nuts, seeds, dried fruit, and fish in which the bones are eaten, e.g. sardines
Iron	Needed to form part of haemoglobin, which gives red blood cells their colour, and allows them to carry oxygen in the blood to body cells	Offal such as liver and kidneys. Other good sources are red meat, oily fish, poultry, green leafy vegetables, beans and lentils, dried fruit, fortified bread and breakfast cereals
Vitamin A	Needed for good eyesight, growth and healthy skin and tissue	Liver, butter, eggs and fish oils. You can also get vitamin A from carotene, vegetables, orange and yellow fruit, and margarine
Vitamin B complex	Needed in the body to transfer and release energy and for the formation of red blood cells	Cereals, meat, fish and dairy products, beans, peas and lentils, yeast and yeast extract
Vitamin C	Makes blood vessels stronger, helps the body heal faster and helps resist infections. It also helps the body absorb iron from food	Oranges, kiwi, blackcurrants, guavas, papayas, peppers, broccoli, brussels sprouts, strawberries, grapefruit, tangerines, mangoes, melons, cauliflower, tomatoes, potatoes, spinach, okra and cabbage
Vitamin D	Needed to help the absorption of calcium for strong bones and teeth	Sunlight. Also in eggs and fatty fish

Calcium

If there is a lack of calcium in our **diet**, the body takes it from our bones instead. This makes bones weak and causes problems in later life such as osteoporosis (weakening of the bones).

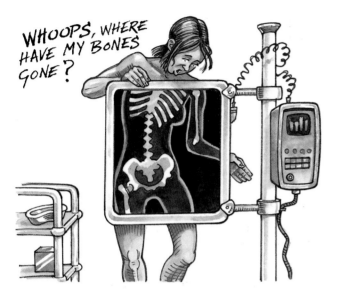

WHOOPS, WHERE HAVE MY BONES GONE?

Iron

Anaemia, caused by lack of iron in the diet, is one of the most common nutritional problems in the world. The symptoms are tiredness, dizziness and weakening of the immune system. Women and children are at greatest risk of developing iron-deficiency anaemia.

Vitamins

There are two groups of vitamins: water-soluble and fat-soluble.

Water-soluble vitamins

Water-soluble vitamins dissolve in water and tend to be passed out of the body every day in urine. This means they are not stored in the body. The other problem is that they can be 'lost' during food preparation. Foods rich in these vitamins should be eaten every day.
- Vitamin B complex: there are several B vitamins, but the ones you need to think about are folic acid and vitamin B12. Folic acid is found in the foods mentioned in the

table as well as in green vegetables. It is an important vitamin for pregnant women and for those planning to become pregnant as low levels of folic acid at conception can increase the risk of a baby being born with spina bifida, a neural tube defect. Vitamin B12 is found mainly in animals or animal products (dairy products and eggs). If someone does not eat these products, such as a vegan, they will lack this vitamin in their diet. However, yeast extract does contain B12.
- Vitamin C: everyone knows that oranges are full of vitamin C, but it is worth knowing what other fruit and vegetables also contain good amounts of this vitamin.

Fat-soluble vitamins

Fat-soluble vitamins are vitamins A, D, E and K. These vitamins can usually be stored in the liver in the body. This means you do not have to eat them every day. You will have enough vitamin E (for skin, heart health and reproduction) and vitamin K (for blood clotting), but you can get deficiencies in the other two.

? Test your knowledge

1 What extra ingredients could you add to bread to increase the iron content?

2 Why is it more important to be concerned with the vitamin C content of food rather than the vitamin A content?

Activity

In pairs or small groups, discuss which ingredients you could add to a spaghetti bolognese recipe to improve the vitamin C content.

Summary

★ Micronutrients are essential for a healthy body.

★ Water-soluble vitamins must be eaten every day.

★ It is easy to improve the micronutrient content of your diet by eating more fruit and vegetables, enough red meat and wholegrain cereals.

The function of ingredients

Introduction to the physical functions of ingredients

In this chapter you will:

★ learn about the physical function of food ingredients.

It is always better to have practical experience of something rather than be told about it in a book or hear it being described by someone. For example, 'It has a smooth, slightly slimy texture, with an initial salty taste and a rich, fishy, exciting aftertaste' might not be your experience of eating a raw oyster!

You need to have practical experience of working with food ingredients so that you can understand the physical properties of basic ingredients. Cakes, bread, pasta and biscuits contain almost the same ingredients. Experimenting with these products will help you to understand ingredients that are used in a lot of food products.

Flour

Flour is a bulk ingredient that forms the structure of a product. Bulk ingredients are often starchy products from cereals. They are also inexpensive. The starch in flour gelatinises when it is heated; this means it absorbs liquid to form a structure. This structure is moist and has a good, open texture, especially if the right amount of raising agent is used.

The protein in flour mixes with liquid to produce gluten. The raising agent stretches this and, when cooked, it coagulates (sets) to produce a stable structure, expanding the gluten and making it rise. When it is cooked, it stays firm.

During cooking, starch on the outside of the food product changes to dextrin and turns a golden-brown colour. This is called dextrinisation.

Sugar

Sugar is not just there to sweeten food products; it is also an inexpensive bulk ingredient. It adds colour to a product and affects the texture. When heated, dry sugar melts and caramelises (turns brown). You only have to think about how crunchy a toffee or sweet can be to realise that this is an important function of sugar.

Sugar also aerates a mixture, which means it increases in size when air is added. When sugar and fat are beaten together (creamed), the crystals of sugar mix with the fat. The air that is beaten into the mixture sticks to the crystals. The fat surrounds the air bubbles and 'traps' them in the mixture.

Sugar is also hydroscopic – it is attracted to water. This means that sugar helps products to stay moist so they keep longer and do not dry out.

Fat

Fat generally improves the flavour and texture of baked products. It has a shortening effect in baked products. This means it produces a crumbly, soft texture rather than being chewy. Fat stops the protein in flour from absorbing liquid and making gluten. It does this by surrounding the flour particles and forming a waterproof coating. Gluten is elastic and stretchy; if it is stopped from forming, the mixture is crumbly and 'short' rather than stretchy and elastic.

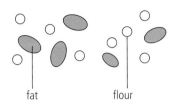

fat   flour

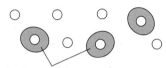

fat forming a waterproof coating around flour

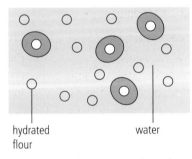

hydrated   water
flour

Fat prevents gluten from forming, making the texture soft and crumbly

Fat also traps air bubbles when beaten or creamed, forming a foam. Fat can do this because it is mouldable and pliable. The addition of sugar also helps foam to form. It also helps to increase the **shelf life** of baked products because fat helps to keep in moisture.

Raising agents

These are added to products to make them rise. Raising agents are gases that expand on heating, pushing up the surrounding mixture. Baking powder is a chemical (man-made) raising agent that produces the gas carbon dioxide. Yeast is a biological (natural) raising agent that also produces carbon dioxide. Other raising agents are air (used in meringues) and steam (used in batters).

Eggs

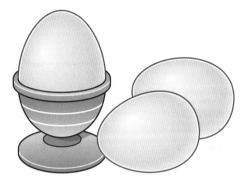

Eggs have many uses in cooking. The four main properties are that eggs:
- coagulate when heated, which means they set – this makes them a good binding agent as they hold dry ingredients together
- foam – the protein in egg white stretches when it is beaten (whisked), trapping air
- aerate mixtures – even when they are mixed with other ingredients, such as sugar and fat in a cake mixture, they trap air
- are a good emulsifier – they stop fats and water separating in the mixture.

Because of their coagulating properties, eggs are also used to glaze baked products.

Activities

1 In pairs or small groups, make small numbers of fairy cakes, each time adding or taking away certain ingredients such as sugar and fat.

2 Carry out sensory analysis to evaluate your products.

Summary

★ Carrying out experiments with basic ingredients used in lots of products will help the understanding of the physical function of ingredients.

★ The physical function of these ingredients can also be considered during product evaluations of existing products.

The function of ingredients

Physical functions of carbohydrates

> **In this chapter you will**
> ★ learn more about the physical function of different flours and sugars.

All the basic ingredients discussed in Chapter 2.4 have different varieties that can be used in food products. These can change the structure and taste of products.

Flour

There are many different types of flour

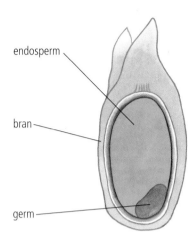

A wheat grain

Wheat flour

Wheat flour is used in baking because of its gluten content. Gluten is a protein that stretches when a raising agent is used and forms a light, airy structure when cooked. Wheat flours can contain different amounts of gluten. Therefore, different wheat flours can be used for different mixtures and cooking processes. They can be classified according to their protein (gluten) content.

Flour	Protein content	Suitability
Strong white flour	High (17%)	Bread, pasta, flaky pastry
White plain or self-raising flour	Medium (10%)	Cakes, biscuits, shortcrust pastry
Soft or cake flour	Low (8%)	Rich cakes, biscuits

Wheat flours can also be classified according to their extraction percentage (how much of the wheat grain is used). A wheat grain consists of 85% endosperm (the white part – mainly starch and some protein), 12% bran (the outside husk – mainly dietary fibre) and 3% wheatgerm (where the new plant begins – contains vitamins).

White flour has an extraction rate of 70–5%, which means 70–5% of the grain has been extracted to make the flour.

Wholemeal or wholewheat flour has an extraction rate of 85–100%. This flour produces closer textured, denser products because the bran and wheatgerm it contains weaken the gluten and prevent it from working properly. The bran also absorbs liquid, so extra liquid is often needed when the flour is used in cooking.

Brown flour is a mixture of white and wholemeal flour. Granary flour is white flour with wholegrains, rye flour and malt extract added. UK law requires brown and white flour to be fortified with nutrients such as vitamin B complex and some minerals that may have been lost during milling.

Other flours

Flour can also be made from other cereals and root crops such as potatoes, rice and rye. These flours can be combined with wheat flour to produce different tasting and textured food products such as potato bread. Rye bread is very dense, has a dark colour and a rich, nutty flavour. These other flours can be used on their own to make bread, but it is only wheat flour, where the protein changes to gluten, that creates an elastic dough that rises easily. These forms of flour may also be used by people with an allergy to wheat.

Sugar

There are many different types of sugar

Sugar comes from sugar beet or sugar cane. The beet or cane is crushed and mixed with water and the liquid boiled to obtain sugar crystals. These crystals are then refined in different ways to produce various white and brown forms.

White sugars

The sugar most commonly used in baked products is caster sugar. This is because this sugar helps with aeration. When sugar is beaten with fat, the air that is beaten in sticks to the sugar crystals and the fat surrounds the air bubbles to trap them inside. Caster sugar has a large number of fine crystals, which means more air bubbles and better aeration. Granulated sugar has fewer, bigger crystals and icing sugar has crystals that are much too small to work in this way.

1 Before being beaten

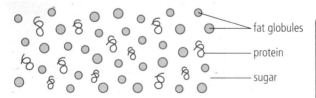

fat globules
protein
sugar

2 After being beaten

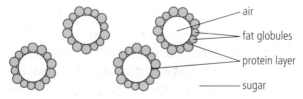

air
fat globules
protein layer
sugar

Using caster sugar helps with aeration

Brown sugars

Some sugars, such as demerara, soft light brown and dark brown, are coloured because some of the molasses (the liquid produced when the sugar crystals are made) are allowed to remain with the crystals. These sugars have a stronger flavour than white sugars, meaning they affect both the flavour and colour of products.

Syrups

Syrups are liquid sugars that attract water. This means they help keep baked products moist and in good condition for a long time.

- Black treacle is made from molasses, the residue from sugar cane refining. It has a strong flavour and is thick, dark and heavy. It is often used in gingerbread and parkin.
- Golden syrup is a refined, light syrup that has had some of the impurities taken out of it. It is sweeter than sugar.
- Honey is made by bees and varies in flavour and colour. This is entirely due to the different flowers the bees have visited for nectar.

? Test your knowledge

1 Explain why a strong flour is needed for pasta.
2 Why does wholemeal flour produce a chewy, dense bread?
3 Why is caster sugar used in meringues?
4 Which sweetener is often used in gingerbread?

✎ Activity

For homework, make bread using different kinds of flour such as white self-raising wheat flour, cake flour and rice flour. What differences do you notice? Write notes about what each type of bread is like, commenting on appearance, texture and taste.

Summary

★ Using different varieties of flour and sugar will affect the final properties of a food product.

The function of ingredients

2.6 Physical functions of raising agents and liquids

> **In this chapter you will**
> ★ understand the physical function of raising agents and liquids in more detail.

Raising agents

Raising agents are added to baked products to make them rise. There are three raising agents that expand on heating to push up the surrounding mixture, making baked products rise: air, steam and carbon dioxide. Chemical and biological raising agents, such as baking powder and yeast, can also be added to the mixture – these also work to produce carbon dioxide.

Air

Adding air to a mixture makes it lighter. Air is a mixture of gases and is added by:

- creaming: when fat and sugar are creamed together, air bubbles become trapped

- whisking and beating: egg white is capable of holding up to seven times its own volume of air because of the way the protein stretches; whole egg also traps a lot of air

- sieving: when flour is sieved, air becomes trapped between its fine particles

- folding and rolling: when flaky and puff pastry is made, air is trapped between the layers

1
press dough to a rectangle and roll it to a strip

2
cut fat into 1cm cubes

3
put fat on two thirds of dough

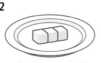

4
fold and roll three times more, adding fat at the folds

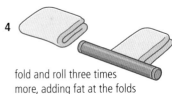

- rubbing in: air is trapped as fat is rubbed into flour when making scones, biscuits and pastry.

Steam

Steam (water in a gaseous state) is produced from the liquid present in a mixture. Water turns to steam when heated to 100°C. Water vapour or steam expands up to 1600 times its original volume. However, steam is often combined with other raising agents because it is slow to react alone. It is also effective only in mixtures that:

- contain a lot of liquid such as batters (Yorkshire puddings), choux pastry (eclairs) or flaky pastry
- are cooked at high oven temperatures such as some breads.

Carbon dioxide

Carbon dioxide (CO_2) can be added to the mixture chemically or biologically:

- chemical raising agents need liquid and heat to produce carbon dioxide
- biological raising agents need liquid, heat, food and time to produce carbon dioxide.

Chemical raising agents

- Baking powder is the most commonly used chemical raising agent. It is a commercial mix of bicarbonate of soda and an acid. These react together to produce carbon dioxide. Cornflour or rice flour is added to the mixture to bulk it up and stop any reaction before use. Baking powder is used in small quantities and must be measured accurately.
- Bicarbonate of soda can be used on its own, but it leaves an unpleasant sharp taste and a yellow colour. It can be used in strong flavoured mixtures, such as gingerbread, or it can be used with an acid such as cream of tartar, sour milk or vinegar.

Biological raising agents

Yeast comes in a variety of forms, such as dried, fast-action dried and fresh

Yeast is a single-cell plant fungus that needs food, warmth and liquid to ferment. It is used in most breads. It uses the flour for food and ferments with the liquid to produce carbon dioxide and alcohol. Yeast needs time to ferment, so bread is left to 'prove'. The dough is left in a warm place and given time for the yeast to multiply, produce carbon dioxide and expand the mixture.

Liquids

One of the functions of liquids is to stick dry ingredients together. Such liquid binding ingredients include:

- egg: used when a rich flavour is required
- water: usually used in products such as bread, pastry and pasta to bind the dry ingredients together. Water is needed to help form gluten in the flour. If enough is used, it also produces steam when heated to help the mixture rise
- milk or yoghurt: used instead of water in bread making. This gives the bread a softer texture and crust, and improves the nutritional value. Milk is used instead of egg in some cake mixtures, such as scones and rock buns, where a bland rather than rich flavour is required. It is often used in biscuit recipes for the same reason.

✎ Activity

In small groups, learn more about the way yeast works by trying this experiment. Dissolve 25 g of fresh yeast in 150 ml of warm water. Divide the mixture between four labelled test tubes. Put a balloon over the top of each test tube. Put the first test tube in a warm place. Add $\frac{1}{2}$ tsp sugar to the other three. Put one of these in a warm place, another in a fridge and the last in a jug of boiling water, making sure none of the water goes into the test tube. Leave the samples for at least 15 minutes. What happened to each sample? Record and discuss your results.

Summary

★ There are three raising agents: air, steam and carbon dioxide.

★ Chemical and biological raising agents both produce carbon dioxide.

★ Chemical raising agents have to be measured carefully.

★ Biological raising agents need time and food to work.

The function of ingredients

> **In this chapter you will:**
> ★ learn that there are ethical and moral issues to be considered when choosing ingredients for a food product and particular **target groups**.

Some **consumers** and manufacturers choose ingredients to use in their food products for reasons other than the physical, sensory or nutritional function that food provides. They choose to think about where the ingredients have come from, when and how they were made, and who made them. This might mean that the ingredients are organic and GM (genetically modified) free, that they are 'fair trade', or simply that they have been supplied by a local farmer.

Manufacturers also choose special ingredients that have been changed so that they behave in a special way needed in a particular product – they are **smart ingredients**.

People make food choices for a variety of reasons

Organic ingredients

Organic is a legally defined term, regulated by the EU. The definition of organic food is that it has been grown on an organic farm where no chemical fertilisers or pesticides have been used. Organic products contain no artificial **additives**. Some people choose to eat organic food because they think ordinary food could be harmful and the way it is produced harms the environment. Others say organic food tastes better and contains more nutrients than standard food because the chemicals affect the taste mechanism and disrupt the natural sugars. There are

those, too, who believe that organic food is no better than ordinary food. Eating organic food can be one way to make sure you do not eat GM food.

GM foods

GM foods are those where the genes have been altered to produce new characteristics. The genes have been taken from one species and transferred to another. For example, the 'antifreeze' gene in Arctic fish has been introduced into tomatoes and strawberries to make them freeze-resistant. Some people say that GM foods could be a solution to the world's food problems. It can make crops resistant to disease, increase the quantity (yield) produced and improve the nutritional value of food. Others say genetic engineering crosses natural species barriers, which could lead to weaknesses, diseases and toxins being produced. They are worried that, once released into the environment, genetic mistakes cannot be recalled or cleaned up.

Fairtrade products

Look for this mark on Fairtrade products

Fairtrade ingredients guarantee a better deal to producers in the developing world. Ingredients are bought direct from product organisations – cutting out the 'middlemen' – which means a stable price that always covers production costs and an extra premium that is used to reinvest into business or community projects. Ethical trading means the basic rights of the employees in developing countries are respected. It is possible to buy a variety of Fairtrade products such as chocolate, fruit, sugar, tea and coffee.

Smart ingredients

Smart ingredients are natural products that have been changed in some way to make them behave in a more useful way. They do not occur naturally – they are the result of new and improved processes (new technology). They are used by food manufacturers in all sorts of ways:

- to make a food behave in a certain way, for example a sauce in a ready meal that stays runny when cold
- to use as an alternative ingredient, for example a meat analogue (a product that has been produced to look and taste like meat such as Quorn) or a fat replacer
- to improve the nutritional content, for example fortified breakfast cereals and Omega 3 egg (see the case study opposite).

Here are some smart ingredients that could be used in baked products (see also page 98):

- sweeteners: there are two basic types:
  - intense sweeteners, such as saccharin and aspartame, which are up to 500 times sweeter than sugar
  - bulk sweeteners, such as sorbitol, which provide the same bulk as sugar in a product
- fat replacers: these are used by food manufacturers; they cannot be bought in supermarkets. One example of a fat replacer is a modified starch that has been produced to give the mouth feel that fat gives without the fat being present. Note that low-fat spreads usually contain less than 30% fat, meaning they are not suitable for baking because the rest of the volume is partially made up of water and air
- functional foods: many products are fortified with a range of different nutrients. For example, white flour has a B vitamin (thiamin) added to raise the content level to those found in wholemeal flour. White flour can also be fortified with a modified starch that increases the NSP (fibre) content. This means that white bread can have the same NSP content as wholemeal bread, but the texture is the same as a standard white loaf.

Sweeteners and low-fat spreads are smart products

Case Study

Columbus eggs

Columbus hens are fed a special **diet** that is more varied than a normal hen's diet. This includes a wider range of seeds and green vegetation. Therefore, Colombus eggs contain less saturated fat, more polyunsaturated fat and a lot more Omega 3, a fatty acid that is essential for a healthy heart.

Activities

1 a Research the range of organic products available in your neighbourhood.

   b Produce a poster describing some of these products.

2 Use the information in this book, any additional information provided by your teacher, and any other sources, such as the Internet, to briefly explain the case for and against the use of GM crops.

Summary

★ Some consumers and manufacturers choose to use organic, fair trade or GM-free products.

★ Some manufacturers source locally produced products to boost the local economy or because consumers demand these kind of products.

★ Some food manufacturers use smart ingredients in their products so that the properties of the product are improved.

The function of ingredients

The different functions of ingredients

In this chapter you will:
★ learn about the choice of and use of food ingredients
★ revise the different functions of ingredients.

There are hundreds of ingredients that are used in food products, but some are used in many products in different ways. Some products are used more than others. For example, think about the two ingredients on this page.

Wheat

Wheat is used in lots of products

Wheat has a bland flavour and the texture can be changed with different processes. It is usually processed into flour, but it can be eaten partially processed in other ways such as couscous, bulgar wheat and ebly.

Flour is used as a bulk ingredient in pasta, bread, cakes, pastry and biscuits because it is a good source of energy. It is also used in sauces for its thickening properties and in savoury snacks such as cheese savouries.

There are several different types of flour:
- wholemeal flour is used when a 'healthy' product is needed as it contains more NSP (fibre)
- strong flour is used for bread to make a stretchy, doughy texture
- finely refined flour is used in sauces so that it does not become lumpy
- duram wheat flour is used for pasta making because it makes a harder flour.

If you mind mapped all the products made out of wheat, there could be thousands. Think of how many different types of biscuit there are, or the various types of bread you can buy such as hot-cross buns, ciabatta, naan, bagettes, wholemeal, brown and granary.

Bananas

Bananas are quite a versatile ingredient

Bananas are used in fewer products as they have a strong flavour, and a distinct texture and sweetness.
- They can be eaten whole as an easy-to-eat and nutritious snack or part of a packed lunch.
- They have high starch content, which means they provide lots of energy – some tennis players eat them to give them energy in long matches.
- Bananas are the base of many smoothies because they make a thick purée.
- They are added to many desserts, drinks and sweets as they add flavour and sweetness. The shape of a banana can create an attractive dessert such as a banana split.
- Bananas are often used in cakes and muffins.
- Bananas are added to fruit salads as they are a soft fruit compared to a crunchy apple.
- Dried bananas give a nice crunchy texture in muesli or other breakfast cereals.

The function of ingredients

Some food ingredients are used more because they carry out important functions. You need to understand these functions to help you understand how and why products

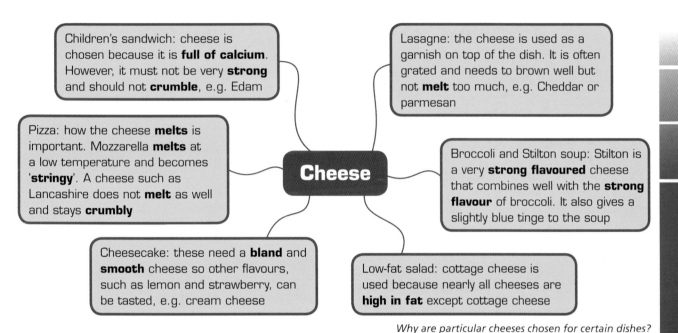

Children's sandwich: cheese is chosen because it is **full of calcium**. However, it must not be very **strong** and should not **crumble**, e.g. Edam

Lasagne: the cheese is used as a garnish on top of the dish. It is often grated and needs to brown well but not **melt** too much, e.g. Cheddar or parmesan

Pizza: how the cheese **melts** is important. Mozzarella **melts** at a low temperature and becomes '**stringy**'. A cheese such as Lancashire does not **melt** as well and stays **crumbly**

Cheese

Broccoli and Stilton soup: Stilton is a very **strong flavoured** cheese that combines well with the **strong flavour** of broccoli. It also gives a slightly blue tinge to the soup

Cheesecake: these need a **bland** and **smooth** cheese so other flavours, such as lemon and strawberry, can be tasted, e.g. cream cheese

Low-fat salad: cottage cheese is used because nearly all cheeses are **high in fat** except cottage cheese

Why are particular cheeses chosen for certain dishes?

are made in a certain way. This will help you during product development work when you are developing your own food products.

Previous chapters have taught you about the:
• sensory function of ingredients
• nutritional function of ingredients
• physical function of ingredients.

It can be difficult to understand the function of ingredients because any one ingredient may have more than one function. Look at the diagram above to help understand these different functions. The words in bold are those that describe either the physical function ('melts', 'crumbles'), the sensory function ('strong', 'bland', 'blue') or the nutritional function of cheese ('high in fat', 'full of calcium').

When you make food products, you need to think about all the different functions each ingredient brings to the product. This is important if you want to develop the product. For example, if you know cheese is high in fat and you want to reduce the fat content, you can alter the amount of cheese you use or the type of cheese you use. But, if you also know it is full of flavour, you may have to add an extra ingredient to compensate for this.

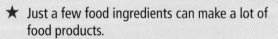
Activities

1 For homework:
  a Look at a range of different food packaging to analyse how often wheat is used in food products. Do the same for another cereal such as maize or rice. Draw a mind map to show all the food products made from wheat.
  b Choose an ingredient that is not used in so many ways such as strawberries. Create a mind map showing all the food products you can think of that include strawberries.

2 a Add to your wheat mind map by including the function of the wheat in the product shown. For example, in cakes, wheat is the bulking ingredient.
  b For each of the functions you have added, identify its purpose. Is it physical, nutritional or sensory? Is it all or one or two of these?

Summary

★ Just a few food ingredients can make a lot of food products.

★ It is important to understand the physical, sensory and nutritional function of these ingredients.

The function of ingredients

Exam questions

1 A bread product to be served with a burger will be developed in a test kitchen.

   a Describe three main ingredients needed to make the bread product. Explain why each ingredient is used.

Ingredients	Why used?

(6 marks)

   b Describe, with reasons, three different ways of developing a basic bread recipe to give more interest and appeal to children.

Development 1	Reason
Development 2	Reason
Development 3	Reason

(6 marks)
(AQA 2003)

2 What is the function of fat in shortcrust pastry? *(3 marks)*
(AQA/NEAB 2001)

3 A manufacturer buys in basic ingredients for the production of cakes and biscuits. Each ingredient has an important use in preparation and cooking.

Ingredient	Use of ingredient in preparation and cooking
Fat	1 It adds flavour
	2 It improves texture
Sugar	
Eggs	
Raising agent	
Flour	

Complete the table to give two reasons for the use of each ingredient in preparation and cooking. An example is given to help you. *(8 marks)*

(AQA/NEAB 1999)

4 A test kitchen has produced a batch of American cherry muffins.

   a Six sensory descriptors could be used to evaluate this product. Two examples have been given for you. Name another four. *(4 marks)*

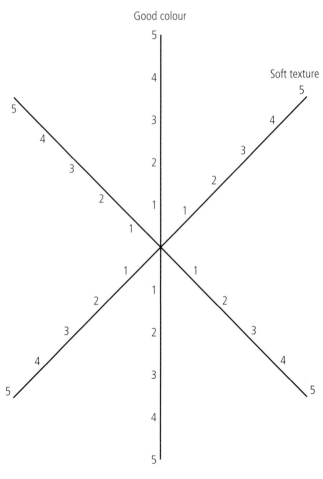

   b The taste panel carry out the evaluation of the muffins under controlled conditions. Explain how this would be done. *(4 marks)*

(AQA/NEAB 1999)

Designing

This section covers the whole design process except research activities, which are looked at in Section 1. The skills shown in this section should be learnt during your course so that they can be used confidently during your coursework.

What's in this section?

★ **3.1** Analysing research and writing an outline specification

★ **3.2** Generating initial ideas

★ **3.3** ICT in designing

★ **3.4** Creative designing

★ **3.5** Concept screening and presentation of ideas

★ **3.6** Developing ideas

★ **3.7** Evaluating ideas and writing a product specification

Analysing research and writing an outline specification

In this chapter you will:

★ learn how to use knowledge gained from research activities to guide design decisions

★ learn how to analyse research and how to write an outline **specification**.

IN MY QUESTIONNAIRE, PEOPLES FAVOURITE SHAPE WAS A RECTANGLE AND FAVOURITE FLAVOUR WAS FRUITY.

THAT ORANGE FLAVORED BISCUIT TASTED NICE BUT I DIDN'T LIKE THE PEANUT ONE.

WHEN I LOOKED ON THE INTERNET I LIKED THE SOUND OF HONEY AND BANANA BISCUITS AND THE WHITE CHOCOLATE CHIP AND RASPBERRY ONES THIS FITS WHAT PEOPLE LIKE TOO.

WHEN WE EXPERIMENTED WITH DIFFERENT FATS THE BUTTER WAS THE BEST FLAVOUR. ADDING OATS GAVE A NICE TEXTURE.

ALL THAT INFORMATION ABOUT NUTRITION WAS INTERESTING. I NEED TO MAKE HEALTHY BISCUITS – THEY MUST HAVE NSP AND VITAMINS IN NOT TOO MUCH SUGAR TOO.

WELL IF I MAKE BISCUITS THEY'VE GOT TO BE VERY TASTY AND HAVE A GOOD COLOUR.

ALL THAT INFORMATION ABOUT NUTRITION WAS INTERESTING. I NEED TO MAKE HEALTHY BISCUITS – THEY MUST HAVE NSP AND VITAMINS IN. NOT TOO MUCH SUGAR.

Analysing research

When you complete research activities such as questionnaires, product evaluations, sensory analysis of existing products or experimenting with certain ingredients, you may have lots of thoughts. You will have found out plenty of information, which has given you loads of ideas. You now need to come to some conclusions. You need to decide how to use the information to help you design a quality product. This is called analysing research.

Here is an example of an analysis of one research activity.

I experimented with different fats and mixtures of fats in shortcrust pastry. I used sensory analysis to evaluate the different kinds of pastry. Six people tasted them.
- Everyone disliked the pastry made with just lard.
- Pastry made from butter was the favourite in terms of taste, but everyone said it was too crumbly.
- The preferred texture was the one made with half margarine and half lard, but the flavour of this pastry was only satisfactory.

This experiment has shown me that:
- my pastry should contain butter
- my pastry might need to include another fat to improve the texture.

I need to carry out further experiments for this **component** of my product.

Analysing means working out what you have learnt and writing down your thoughts from this learning on paper. It focuses your thoughts and makes you channel ideas in the right direction. An easy way to analyse research is to:

- consider one piece of research at a time and briefly explain what you did
- first, work out what you have found out that is relevant
- next, work out how you will use this information in your designing.

Coursework

You must analyse all research activities to gain a good grade. An outline specification that reflects this analysis is also essential.

Outline specification

When you have analysed all the research activities you have carried out, the next step is to use these ideas and thoughts to write an outline specification. This kind of specification can also be called a general specification, a design specification, an initial specification or design criteria.

A specification is a series of statements that describe the possibilities and restrictions of a product. These statements give certain conditions that the product must meet. A specification is a list of things explaining what you want your product to be like.

A specification should be written in bullet points for easy reference. When you evaluate the products you have made, you will look at the outline specification to check if the product matches it. You will check that the product you have made is what you wanted the product to be like.

An outline specification should include the following points:
- the **target group** the product is aimed at
- a description of the product or kind of products: their purpose and function
- what they should look and taste like (including texture and weight or size)
- the kind of ingredients you will include
- where they will be stored and for how long, including any safety points
- any special nutritional requirements
- costs
- environmental issues such as packaging.

Here are two examples. Remember that the statements have been decided because the analysis of research suggested them. They are based on the results of actual research.

Example of an outline specification for a biscuit
- *A healthy biscuit aimed at children.*
- *Looks colourful.*
- *Chewy, slightly crunchy texture.*
- *Fruity taste, but not too strong.*
- *Medium size – about 10 in a packet.*
- *Shelf life of at least one month – so not too moist.*
- *Priced less than £1, so cost no more than 30p per 10 to make.*
- *Lots of fibre, low in sugar and with added vitamins.*
- *Minimal packaging – clear to see biscuits, paperboard base.*
- *Suitable to be made in large quantities.*

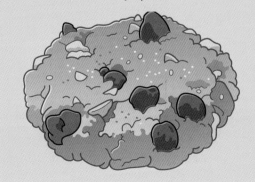

Example of an outline specification for a savoury main course suitable for a special diet
- *A savoury main course suitable for a healthy option range.*
- *Looks colourful, full of flavour and with a variety of textures.*
- *About 300 g – suitable for one person.*
- *Shelf life of ten days at chilled temperatures.*
- *Priced less than £3.*
- *No more than 5 g of fat per 100 g of food.*
- *Lots of fibre and low in salt.*
- *Minimal packaging – paperboard outer and coated paperboard inner, suitable for microwave or oven.*
- *Suitable to be made in large quantities.*

Some statements in an outline specification can be specific and some can be more open. For example, a 'fruity taste' suggests some kind of fruit should be used, so this point is specific. On the other hand, 'full of flavour' is more open, meaning that all kinds of ingredients can be used to create this flavour.

From the outline specification you can think of suitable ideas that match up to all the statements in the specification.

Activities

1 Analyse a research activity you have completed. Try to write a list of at least five points showing the information you have gained.

2 Write an outline specification for a Christmas bread. Will it be savoury or sweet? What size and shape will it be? Will it include some surface decoration?

Summary

★ Analysing research activities helps you to work out what you have learnt from these activities.

★ Writing an outline specification, using the information gained from research, will help with design ideas and decisions.

Designing

3.2 Generating initial ideas

> In this chapter you will:
> ★ learn how to use an outline **specification** to generate initial ideas.

Writing an outline specification helps focus your thoughts and ideas on the products. You now need to write down these ideas.

Mind mapping ideas

One way to come up with ideas is to mind map your thoughts. This means drawing a diagram to show your thoughts. Mind mapping is often best done in groups of people working together to think of lots of ideas.

If the specification is for a biscuit, you could mind map existing biscuits. The next step could be to put two or three flavours together to get even more ideas such as apple, cinnamon and chocolate, or honey, oats and banana.

Sometimes it is easier to break down the task of 'designing ideas' into smaller parts. Different parts of a specification

can be considered one at a time or certain ingredients can be considered for a particular product, for example 'What type of pastry should be used?', 'What kind of starchy food?' The mind map below shows how this has been done for the specification of 'colourful' biscuits.

The example on the opposite page shows a mind map for different ingredients in one product – a lasagne for a multicultural ready meal.

Mind mapping in this way will help you sort through all your ideas and help you to come up with just a few themes that best fit the outline specification to test and trial. This technique is a good way to help you get started with ideas and designing, but there are other ways you could try.

Looking at existing recipes

Another way to get ideas is to look through recipe books (see the example on the opposite page) or at recipes on the Internet. You need to be systematic, making sure the recipe matches the outline specification. Try to use UK sites so that the measurements are easy to understand. As you look in books, write down the name of the product and the page and book you are looking at so you know where to find the recipe if you want to use it.

Mood boards

Mood boards are another way to trigger design ideas. They consist of lots of images of products or ingredients. These can come from magazines, the internet, or even clipart. They can also include some sketches. In industry, mood boards are used as part of a presentation about ideas. As you will not verbally present your ideas, you need to add your thoughts to the mood board. For example:

'This bread is a really interesting shape. I like the use of herbs on top for presentation. Will it be difficult to produce the same shape again and again?'.

A good place to start looking for ideas is in food magazines and leaflets. Do not forget that you must annotate (label) the images you find. For example, you might annotate an image of a colourful layered dessert as follows:

'This layered dessert has very distinctive layers, with the orange and purple layers contrasting with the cream layers. I must try to create a really colourful dessert.'

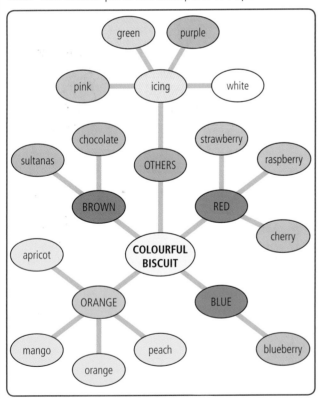

'Colourful' biscuits mind map

Lasagne mind-map – each component part is considered

Spiced Star Biscuits

2 tbsp thin honey
25g (1oz) unsalted butter
50g (2oz) light muscovado sugar
finely grated zest of ½ lemon
finely grated zest of ½ orange
225g (8oz) self-raising flour
1 tsp ground cinnamon
1 tsp ground ginger
½ tsp freshly grated nutmeg
pinch of ground cloves
pinch of salt
1 tbsp finely chopped candied peel
50g (2oz) ground almonds
1 large egg, beaten
1½ tbsp milk

TO DECORATE
150g (5oz) icing sugar
silver sugar balls

makes about 35
preparation: 15 minutes, plus chilling
cooking time: 15–20 minutes, plus cooling
per biscuit: 50 cals; 2g fat; 7g carbohydrate

1 Put the honey, butte
small pan and stir over
melted and the ingredie
2 Sift the flour, spices
then add the choppe
almonds. Add the me
milk, and mix until the c
3 Knead the dough br
clingfilm and chill for at
4 Roll out the dough c
5mm (¼ inch) thickne
5cm (2 inch) cutter, and
5 Bake at 180°C (160
minutes or until just beg
Transfer the biscuits to
airtight tin for up to 1 w
6 To decorate, mix t
warm water to make a
the biscuits with icing a
you like, then decorate
icing on the plain bisc
illustrated). Allow the
biscuits in an airtight c

Ginger Biscuits

125g (4oz) golden syrup
50g (2oz) dark muscovado sugar
50g (2oz) butter, plus extra to grease
finely grated zest of 1 orange
2 tbsp orange juice
175g (6oz) self-raising flour
1 tsp ground ginger

makes 24
preparation: 15 minutes
cooking time: about 12 minutes,
    plus cooling
per biscuit: 55 cals; 2g fat;

1 Put the golden syr
and juice into a heavy-b
until melted and evenly
2 Leave the mixture t
flour with the ginger. M
3 Put small spoonfuls
greased large baking s
to allow room for spre
fan oven) mark 4 for 1
are golden brown.
4 Leave on the baki
carefully transfer to a
airtight tin for up to 5 c

Existing recipes can help you with ideas

Coursework

You will need to generate a wide range of design ideas that match the outline specification. This is one of the most important parts of coursework.

Activities

1 Draw a mind map to show any extra ingredients that could be added to a tomato soup to add colour and flavour.

2 Create a moodboard to help you with ideas for a new Chinese stir fry recipe. Add notes and sketches to the images you have found.

Summary

★ There are different ways of getting started with designing. Mind mapping, looking at recipes and creating mood boards are ways to help you to create initial ideas.

ICT in designing

In this chapter you will:

★ learn how to use nutritional analysis and spreadsheet programs for costing, to help with design decisions.

ICT is a useful tool for many areas of food technology. It can be used to help with design ideas, but other ICT packages are available to make filtering ideas easier.

Nutritional analysis programs

There are many nutritional analysis programs and they can be used in several ways:

- to look at the individual ingredients to see what nutrients they would add to a product
- to look at a complete recipe to see if you are happy with its nutritional content

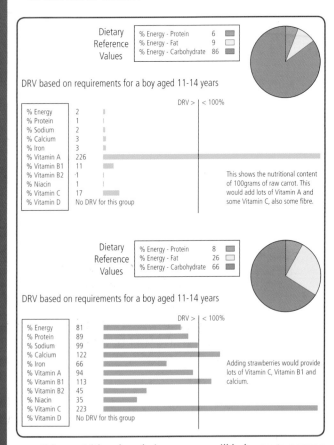

Using nutritional analysis programs will help you to narrow down your ideas – for example when considering ingredients to add to muffins

- to compare several recipe ideas before you choose some to trial.

Costing food products

Cost is important when you are designing products for sale. There is no point in designing and making a food product that is too expensive for people to buy and that makes no **profit** for the company. You have to calculate the cost of ingredients and the likely selling price.

This is easy to do if you use a computer program such as Microsoft Excel. A spreadsheet can be set up with formulas to do the mathematical calculations for you. You can then change the ingredients and see how this affects the total price. Visit www.nutrition.org.uk to look at a selection of costing templates ready for you to use.

Finding the cost of ingredients

If you do not know the cost of the ingredients for your product, you can use the Internet and online shopping sites to find out.

The cost of different ingredients is important. Compare the following prices for three different fruits that could be used in a fruit muffin. Go to www.heinemann.co.uk/hotlinks for more information.

You can see from this example how using more expensive ingredients, such as strawberries or blueberries, would greatly increase the total cost of the fruit muffins.

Fruit	Price (£/kg)
Apples	1.89
Strawberries	6.56
Blueberries	19.92

Working out the selling price

A simple costing sheet that uses formulas will work out the total cost of a recipe. You then need to work out the portion cost. However, the selling price of a food product should take account of more than just the ingredients. Other costs will be:

- packaging

- advertising and **marketing**
- labour
- factory and energy costs
- distribution costs (transport)
- retailers' (shopkeepers') costs.

As well as these costs, a profit also needs to be made! The pie chart below shows the average breakdown of a food company's costs. You could use this as a rough guide to work out the selling price of your food product once you know the cost per portion of ingredients.

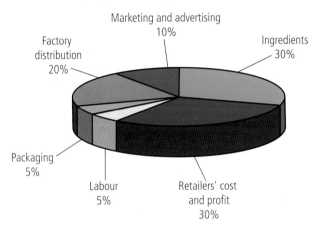

Marketing and advertising 10%

Factory distribution 20%

Ingredients 30%

Packaging 5%

Labour 5%

Retailers' cost and profit 30%

The cost of ingredients is only part of the food manufacturer's selling cost

A single-tier christening cake

A cake with a computer-generated design

Bulk buying ingredients

Food manufacturers can buy ingredients at lower prices than supermarket prices. They buy in bulk. On average, ingredients cost 25–30% less if bought in bulk. You must reduce your cost of ingredients by this amount so that when you work out your selling price it will be realistic.

Special situations for using ICT

ICT can be used in some situations to help design and make a quality product without high levels of practical skills being used. The christening cake in the photo uses highly skilled and expensive workers who are experienced in piping and modelling with sugar paste. The other cake is easy and cheap to produce because it uses a computer to design the picture on the top. The picture is printed onto edible paper using edible ink. It is then stuck onto the icing using a little water.

Coursework

Nutritional analysis and costing are useful to help with design proposals and their development. They also allow you to use appropriate ICT skills.

Activities

1 Use a nutritional analysis program to make a healthy option cake. Experiment with the fat or sugar content of the cake.

2 Use a spreadsheet costing sheet to analyse the different toppings you could add to a pizza to see how this will affect the price.

Summary

★ ICT is a useful tool for some situations. It helps to filter design ideas.

Designing

Creative designing

In this chapter you will
★ learn skills that will help you to be creative in your designing.

Case Study

Heston Blumenthal

Heston Blumenthal

Heston Blumenthal is a 37-year-old self-taught chef who runs The Fat Duck pub bistro in Berkshire. In 2004, his bistro was named as the second-best restaurant in the world (the best in Europe) by *Restaurant* magazine. Mr Blumenthal opened his bistro nine years ago and originally served traditional French provincial dishes. However, he soon threw out the rulebook and began experimenting. His menu now includes:
• egg and bacon ice cream

• snail porridge
• salmon poached with liquorice
• sardine on toast sorbet
• blackcurrant and green peppercorn jelly.

These may not sound very nice, but Mr Blumenthal must be doing something right! His restaurant is one of only three in the UK to get three Michelin stars. Here is his explanation of how he first created his egg and bacon ice cream, which came about because of his interest in 'flavour encapsulation' – capturing the intensity of flavours from ingredients:

'One day I overcooked the egg custard for an ice cream so that it practically became scrambled. I puréed it and made an ice cream from it, which had an immense eggy flavour because of the single egg molecules. But egg by itself was not particularly pleasant. Which was when I decided to see if I could incorporate the sweet tones of smoked bacon into an egg ice cream. Boy, did it work.'

Not all of us can be such imaginative and innovative chefs as Mr Blumenthal. But we can use certain techniques to help us become more creative in our designing. We need to think about putting ingredients together that have not been combined before in food products.

New food products

The food industry uses lots of ways to get different, wacky, imaginative, sensible and creative ideas to help make new products. Each year nearly 10,000 new food and drink products are launched in the UK. The failure rate for these is high – around 90% do not continue to be sold. New products are developed to:
• respond to people's changing tastes
• compete against other companies
• increase profits
• replace products that no longer sell well.

As you already know, one way to get new ideas is to mind map products, ingredients or sections of a product. Another way is to look at existing products in the UK and worldwide. The food industry also gets new ideas from:
• analysing trends in **consumers'** eating habits (by using information gathered from supermarket checkouts)
• competition entries in magazines
• recipes from famous restaurants and their chefs
• ethnic foods from the growth in travel overseas such as Thai curries, Mexican chillis, and Morrocan stews
• government guidelines such as the targets for good health of five portions of fruit and vegetables a day

- modifying existing products for specific **target groups** such as gluten- and nut-free
- health trends such as low-fat meals
- inventors, who sell ideas
- fashion trends (food can follow trends, like clothes and shoes). There is a general trend towards more snack type foods rather than large meals.
- a new ingredient or process that has been developed or a new food that has become available (dragon fruit from Thailand has been used in a new fruit smoothie).

Coursework

Original, creative design proposals should help you to achieve a high grade.

Summary

★ Creative design activities will help you to produce original, imaginative ideas.

Activities

Creative techniques – carry out at least one of the activities below to learn about some of the creative techniques you can use.

1 Design a breakfast pasty.
   a Using a large piece of paper, write down all the different foods you could eat at breakfast. Think about not just a cooked breakfast, but foods like marmalade, orange juice and brown sauce as well.
   b Cut up the piece of paper so each food is on a separate label (as an alternative use Post-it notes).
   c Mix all the food labels up and work out interesting combinations of two, three or four foods together.
   d Choose the best four combinations and compare them with those of others in the class. Who has produced the most interesting combinations? Do you all agree on which is the best one?

2 Use some existing desserts, such as the ones shown here, to inspire your imagination in designing a layered sweet pie.

   The pies opposite have interesting names and interesting layers.
   a Think of an interesting name for a dessert.
   b Decide on the ingredients and layers to include in your dessert.

3 Apricots are used in a traditional Morrocan lamb stew.
   a Write a list of different fruits, meats and vegetables that could be used in a stew.
   b Experiment with different combinations to produce a 'new stew'!

Lemon meringue pie, Banoffi pie and Mississippi mud pie

Designing

3.5 Concept screening and presentation of ideas

> **In this chapter you will:**
> ★ **learn how to sort through initial ideas and select a few to test and trial.**
> ★ **learn how to present these ideas.**

Concept screening

Concept screening is a technique used in the food industry to sort through all initial design ideas and help come up with just a few to test and trial. It is the process of filtering ideas so that only the most suitable products are developed and produced. Concept screening helps to focus design thinking, only developing products that are needed. You will understand this technique more if you look at the two examples on this page. One shows the concept screening process for a student who is designing a multicultural vegetarian dish. The other shows a student 'seiving' ideas of extra ingredients to add to a healthy savoury bread.

Concept screening is a bit like using a sieve in your brain. You work out which ideas are best (those that go through the sieve) and the 'silly', complicated, expensive, unhealthy or boring ideas get left behind in the sieve. The next step for this student after the sieving process is to design a range of breads using these ingredients.

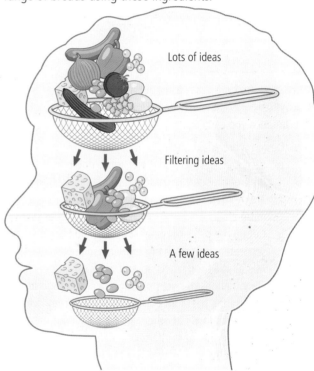

Sieving of ideas for a healthy savoury bread

Lots of ideas	Chilli beans, tofu burgers, curry, couscous, noodles, rice dishes, spring rolls, pulses, pasta, soya products, Quorn™, cheese

Reject Quorn™ and tofu – too expensive.	Reject curry and cheese – don't appeal.	Reject – pulses, chilli beans, spring rolls, soya products, burgers, pasta – too dull and many products already on sale.

A few ideas	Noodles, rice, couscous

Reject rice – reheating problems.	Noodle dishes	Reject couscous – not popular Why? – modern, appeals to teenagers, cheap and different.

Ideas	Stir fry noodles with vegetables, sweet and sour noodles, noodle and vegetable soup, Thai-style vegetables

Reject all but Thai-style vegetables with noodles – came out best in tasting panel.

Develop Thai-style vegetables with noodles

Concept screening for a multicultural vegetarian dish

Presentation of ideas

Once you have selected a few ideas, it is best if you present them visually. This helps you to think about the ingredients you will include, together with the colour, shape and size of the final product.

A visual image does not always mean a beautifully drawn, coloured and annotated picture of each idea. This would take up too much time when you should be making. However, do remember to justify your design ideas against the outline **specification**. This means explaining why you have chosen your ideas and why they fit the specification.

A range of drawing techniques could be used, depending on the product. All drawing of food is best done freehand rather than using rulers and set squares.

Pencil sketches

Simple pencil sketches could be used to start with to help visualise ideas. Simple shading techniques could be used.

Scale view

Because the ingredients are small and distributed all over the bread, a **scale view** is used to illustrate the bread. A scale view is a small square (or circle) showing a close-up of the product. The image is enlarged at a ratio of 5 to 1 to make it easier to draw and identify the ingredients used. Scale views would also be suitable for products with sauces – again, a lot of small ingredients are distributed over a large area.

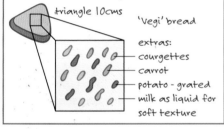

triangle 10cms

'Vegi' bread

extras:
- courgettes
- carrot
- potato - grated
- milk as liquid for soft texture

Isometric projection

Some food products are best shown as **isometric projections** (3D drawings). In these drawings, horizontal lines are at a 30° angle to show three sides. This makes the drawing look more realistic. Products that are a special shape, such as a section of pie, quiche, flan or kebab, are best drawn in this way.

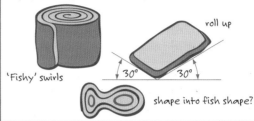

'Fishy' swirls

roll up

30° 30°

shape into fish shape?

Cross section

A **cross-section** is used for this breakfast calzone bread as the filling is contained within the bread. The only way to show the whole product – the inside as well as the outside – is to draw a cross-section. Cross-sections can be exploded views, where each layer is drawn separately.

Breakfast calzone folded over pizza trype bread cross section

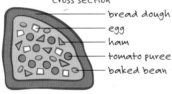

- bread dough
- egg
- ham
- tomato puree
- baked bean

Orthographic projection

Orthographic projection is used here because if all the ingredients are on top of a product, as with this tomato and cheese circle, a bird's eye view is appropriate. Other examples where this would be appropriate are decorated cakes and some biscuits. A cross-section or side view are also included.

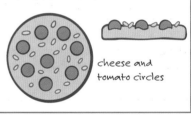

cheese and tomato circles

These drawings, for bread ideas, show a variety of different techniques

Do:

- label your drawings
- draw rough freehand sketches with some colour added
- not spend hours drawing ideas.

You do not need to sketch all your ideas – decide which ones to draw by identifying those that best match the outline specification.

Coursework

You do not have time to trial and make all your ideas, so you must work out the most suitable ideas to trial. You will need to screen, or sort through, your ideas to identify those that best match the outline specification.

Activity

Complete a design sheet showing your ideas for a product. Try to draw two or three different sketches to illustrate your ideas clearly.

Summary

★ Concept screening is a method that reduces many initial ideas into just a few suitable ones.

★ Drawing a few of these ideas will help with design decisions.

Designing

In this chapter you will:
★ learn about the different ways to trial ideas
★ learn how to model using **prototypes**.

When you are at the stage of having a few good ideas that match the outline **specification**, you need to make them in order to test and trial them. There are two different ways of doing this (see table below).

Modelling is often the best way to trial ideas, especially if you have made the product before or have experience of the different processes involved. Looking at these examples of ways to model using prototypes will help with understanding.

Lemon meringue pie

1 Make a basic custard sauce. Divide it into four bowls
and add four different flavourings. For example:
   a Lemon – juice and zest
   b Orange – juice and zest
   c Banana – mashed
   d Blackcurrant – puréed.
      Either taste the different custards or put them into small pastry cases, add meringue on top, cook and taste.

2 Make different pastry as a base.
   a Try different methods – shortcrust, rough puff or suet.
   b Try different fats and combinations of fats in shortcrust pastry.
   c Try alternative bases to pastry – biscuit (different varieties) or sponge (different flavours).

3 Try different methods of making meringue.
   a Make a basic meringue mixture and divide it into three bowls. Leave one as it is, add vinegar to the next and cornflour to the last. Cook the meringues and taste them.
   b Make meringue using three different methods – French, Italian and Swiss.
   c Flavour the meringue with ground nuts, chocolate, etc.

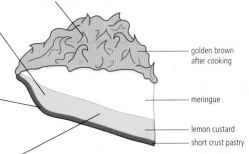

golden brown after cooking

meringue

lemon custard

short crust pastry

4 Make small amounts of the custard sauce using different starches to thicken – cornflour, wheat flour, arrowroot and a modified (smart) starch. Chill and freeze these sauces. Test, when defrosted, after three and seven days.

Method	Advantages of this method	Disadvantages of this method
1 Use a recipe for each idea and make these ideas, one at a time	• You have experience of making the whole product and get a good idea of its overall taste, texture and appearance • You can work out how it needs to be changed to improve it	• You spend a lot of time making each individual product rather than experimenting with the ingredients in a product
2 Model ideas using prototypes – the first versions of a product, used for testing, development and evaluation. Try out several different versions of the product at a time or model one part of it (make small quantities of each idea)	• You can focus on one particular part of a product and work out the best ingredients or process to use • You use the same time to make several ideas, time is saved overall	• If you have not made the product before, you do not know what it tastes and looks like

The two different ways to develop ideas

Curry

Make small quantities – use three or four saucepans to make several variations at a time.

1 Different meats – beef, chicken, lamb or pork.
2 For a vegetable curry, use potato and cauliflower as a base and then add different variations of extra vegetables – peas and sweetcorn, green beans and peppers, ochra and mangetout.
3 Do not use curry powder – investigate different spices used for Indian curries, or Thai and Chinese curries.
4 Use different quantities of hot spices used in a curry (ginger, cayenne pepper, chilli powder) to decide on the ideal quantities.
5 Try other ingredients such as the liquid used. Make a basic mixture of meat and spices. Divide into three saucepans and add water to one, tinned chopped tomatoes to another and coconut milk to the third.

Experimenting with ingredients

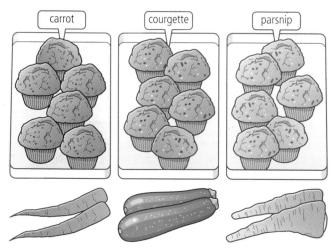

Trial different vegetables that could be used to make cakes healthy – carrot (a well-known cake), courgette and parsnip.

Grate or dice the vegetables. Try out individual flavours or combinations. Make sure you label the prototypes before they go into the oven as all cakes turn brown when cooked!

These are just three examples of how to model using prototypes or how to experiment with ingredients. Other ways could include:

- bread: use one mix of extra ingredients, such as tomato purée and grated cheese, and trial where to put the ingredients – kneaded into the dough or as a layer folded in; different methods of decoration – egg glaze, sugar glaze, seeds, iced, coloured icing
- shepherd's pie: try different mashed potato toppings, either flavoured (onion, garlic, cheese, herb) or presentation (piped, grated cheese, breadcrumbs)
- soup: chunky, processed, half processed and half chunky
- samosas: deep fried, shallow fried or oven baked
- biscuits: different thicknesses or sizes; different sizes of added ingredients such as grated or diced apple, chocolate chunks, chips or grated; add high fibre ingredients such as wholemeal flour or oats; try different quantities of sugar and fat
- stir-fry: different alternative proteins (Quorn, TVP, tofu); different vegetables or sauces (simple soya sauce, sweet and sour, Thai, black bean).

You may be able to think of many more examples. The important thing is to make ideas in the most suitable way so that you can work out which ones are most suitable for developing further.

Coursework

Developing a design solution to match a specification is perhaps the most important part of your coursework. Therefore, showing development work, preferably through modelling, is essential for a good grade.

Activity

Plan the way you will develop a product. Make sure you include some modelling of prototypes in your work.

Summary

★ It is useful to develop ideas using prototypes as this saves time and gives you a wide choice of solutions.

Designing

3.7 Evaluating ideas and writing a product specification

In this chapter you will:
★ learn how to use evaluation techniques to make the right decisions
★ learn how to write a product **specification**.

Evaluations are all about making judgements. They help you decide what to do next. They are an important part of designing and making, and should be done at all stages of the design process, not just when you have made your final product.

Summative and formative evaluations

An evaluation at the end of the design process is a summative evaluation. It works out if the product and processes have been successful. On-going evaluations during the design process are called formative evaluations. You need to complete formative evaluations at every stage of your designing and making so that they can be used to help form the final product.

Evaluating is similar to analysing in that it is putting your thoughts down on paper. You evaluate in your head all the time.

Now what pizza shall I have? I didn't like tuna and sweetcorn last time I was here, but Sam had the ham and mushroom one and that looked nice. Shall I have that one or shall I try something different? I wonder what an artichoke tastes like? Maybe I'll have that one instead.

While you are eating food, you are thinking about how much you like it and whether you would eat it again.

Writing an evaluation

Completing written evaluations means:
• writing down your and other people's views on the product – **sensory evaluation**
• including a check against the outline specification – what you wanted the product to be like
• including details about how you could improve the product.

Write several bullet points for each of the following sections:
1 Explain why you have made the product.
2 Comment on the processes you carried out to make the product and how the making of your product went. What did you find difficult? What was easy? How easy would it be to mass produce this product. You will use this information to help you if you develop the product and make it again.
3 Comment in detail on how your dish turned out using a range of descriptive words. Work out what type of analysis you could use, such as descriptive, preference or discrimination tests. You could use charts and graphs to show the results. This should be the longest section of your evaluation.
4 Explain how the product does or does not match the outline specification. You could use a nutritional analysis program to help you, if appropriate for your product.
5 Explain how you could improve (modify or adapt) this product if you made it again – this should match the comments made about the product.

Product specification

An evaluation will help you to refine an outline specification into a product specification. It helps you to be more precise about what you want a particular product to be like. This will be the specification for your final product.

If you look at the example of an outline specification for a biscuit on the next page, you can now see how it can be developed into a product specification for a particular fruity cookie after you have tested and trialled some ideas.

When you are ready to make the product again, you will have a clear and detailed list of what you want your product to be like.

Outline specification for a biscuit
- A healthy biscuit aimed at children.
- Looks colourful.
- Chewy, slightly crunchy texture.
- Fruity taste, but not too strong.
- Medium size – about 10 in a packet.
- Shelf life of a least one month – so not too moist.
- Priced less than £1, so cost no more than 30p per 10 to make.
- Lots of fibre, low in sugar and with added vitamins.
- Minimal packaging – clear to see biscuits, paperboard base.
- Suitable to be made in large quantities.

Product specification for a biscuit
- A healthy biscuit aimed at children.
- Looks golden brown with red pieces.
- Chewy, soft texture from the biscuit and strawberries, with crunchy bits from the banana.
- Fruity taste – a mix of strawberry and banana.
- Rectangular shape, 80 mm × 50 mm × 15mm.
- 8 or 10 in a packet, depending on cost.
- Shelf life of a least one month – so not too moist.
- Priced less than £1, so cost no more than 30p per 10 to make.
- Lots of fibre from oats and fruit, low in sugar and a good source of vitamins B and C.
- Minimal packaging – clear to see biscuits, paperboard base. Some kind of fruit logo showing fruit content.
- Suitable to be made in large quantities.

- A product specification is for one product only. It can have a more detailed description of the appearance, texture and taste because it is for one product rather than a few products.
- The size, weight and nutritional content can be more precise.
- Other points can include more detail or be altered.

Modifications

An evaluation also helps you to work out how you could modify your product to improve it if or when you make it again. Here is part of an evaluation for a savoury pie.

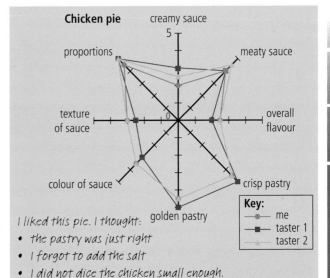

Chicken pie

I liked this pie. I thought:
- the pastry was just right
- I forgot to add the salt
- I did not dice the chicken small enough.

Taster 1 said:
- it was too bland – more seasoning needed
- the meat would be better in smaller pieces
- the sauce was too creamy.

Taster 2 said:
- I could add some vegetables to make it colourful.

When this product was made again, some modifications were made. The chicken was diced smaller, salt and pepper were added, 100 ml of the milk was used instead of cream and four **prototypes** were made with different vegetables added.

Coursework
You need to test and evaluate the making you have carried out and show how you can improve your products. This will help you to produce a detailed product

Activity
Complete an evaluation for a product you have trialled. Ask for other people's opinions. Use sensory analysis and comment on how easy or difficult the product was to make. Include ways you could improve your product.

Summary
★ You should evaluate every product or prototype you make so that you make the right decision for the next stage in the design process.

Exam questions

1 A manufacturer wishes to develop a lunch-time snack product. The general design criteria for this product are that it must:
- have an edible casing
- have a savoury filling
- be hand-held
- be sold in individual portions
- be able to be eaten hot or cold.

a With the aid of labelled sketches, give two different product ideas that satisfy the general design criteria. Do not draw the packaging.

Design Idea 1	Design Idea 2

(6 marks)

b Choose one of your product ideas for the manufacturer to develop. Explain in detail why you have chosen this idea for the manufacturer to develop.
(4 marks)

c Give a product specification for the casing. *(5 marks)*
(AQA/NEAB 2001)

2 A manufacturer wishes to extend the range of ready prepared pizza products. The test kitchen works to the following design criteria. The successful product will:
- be a pizza product
- use fresh vegetables
- be served in individual portions
- be eaten hot or cold
- have a variety of textures.

a With the aid of notes and sketches, produce two different design ideas which meet the design criteria. Do not draw any packaging.

Design Idea 1	Design Idea 2

(8 marks)

b Choose one of your design ideas for the manufacturer to develop. Explain in detail how your chosen design idea meets the design criteria. *(4 marks)*

c Write a product specification for your chosen design idea. *(5 marks)*
(AQA 2004)

4 Making food products commercially

This section covers all the industrial practices involved in food manufacture. You need to understand these so that you can show how the products you design could be made commercially.

What's in this section?

Making food products commercially

In this chapter you will:

★ start to learn about **systems**, controls and feedback.

Systems

A system is a collection of things (objects and/or activities) that work together to perform a task. Every system has three parts:

- inputs – things that go into a system
- process – what happens to everything in the system
- outputs – the end product.

Every time you make a food product, you complete a food production system. For example, when you make bread, you complete a system.

Controls

Controls are used to make sure the system works properly. Controls are different checks and procedures that are built into a system. You automatically use controls when you are making your bread.

- You use clean equipment and ingredients. You clean your hands using antibacterial soap so that your bread will be safe to eat, preventing food safety problems.
- You use the correct flour to make a doughy, stretchy bread.
- You use digital scales to weigh out dry ingredients and a measuring jug for liquids.
- You knead for at least ten minutes to stretch the gluten.
- You let the dough rest (prove) for at least 30 minutes so that the yeast can ferment.
- You do not put the bread into the oven until it has doubled in size.
- You bake the bread at the correct temperature and for the correct time.
- You cool the loaf on a rack so that no condensation forms.
- You taste the bread to see if it has been successful.

You are using measuring, temperature, time, visual, safety and sensory controls. These are **quality controls**. They make sure you produce a good quality food product.

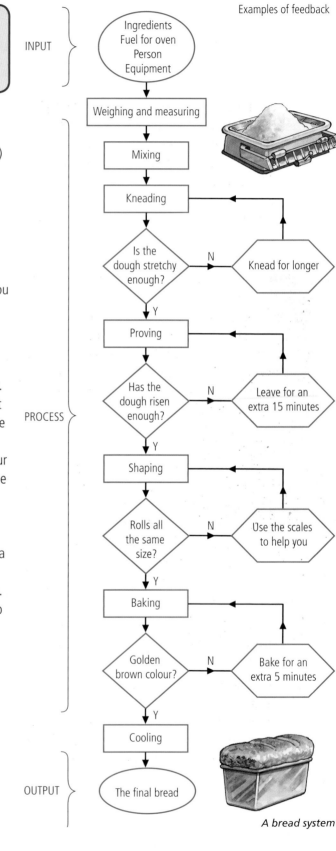

A bread system

Feedback

Feedback means checking on what is happening. It provides information or evidence while the system is working.

You carry out feedback when you make food. For example, when making bread: are the ingredients the right weight? Is the temperature of the liquid too hot? Has the dough risen enough? When making chicken curry you need to check you have diced the meat to the right size. You measure the spices carefully if you want the curry to taste the same as last time. Have you cooked it long enough so that the chicken is safe to eat?

Feedback involves checking that the controls are working. It is reinforcing the system. You might then make a decision to change the process so that you make a better quality product. When making bread, for example, you might decide that the dough needs to prove for an hour or you might think that the bread needs five minutes longer in the oven as the colour is not right. Feedback can also be used at the end of the system: has this product been successful?

Different systems

The food industry uses different production systems depending on the type and number of products to be made. These different systems are called **one-off production**, **batch production** and **mass production** systems. Different systems use varying numbers of people and different sizes and amounts of equipment. In general, the bigger the quantity of food products to be made, the more equipment and less people are used.

One-off production is when just one product is made, usually using a skilled worker. These products are usually expensive.

In batch production, products are made in batches when a specific quantity is needed – for example 200 cakes or 100 loaves of bread. The machinery on the production line can usually be adapted easily so that, for example, different kinds of cakes or bread can be made using the same equipment.

Mass production is often fully automated, using machines purpose-built for the production process. A large number of products are made at the same time, often using a conveyor belt to move the product along the production line.

□ Coursework

Use the information in this chapter to help you consider industrial practices, systems and controls. When doing your coursework project, you will need to show that you have thought about and used industrial practices, systems and controls. Use the information in this chapter to help you.

✎ Activity

Write a system, like the one on the previous page, for a tray of ten double chocolate chip cookies. Include controls and feedback where appropriate.

Summary

★ A system is a way to describe making a food product.

★ Quality controls are used to make sure the system works properly.

One-off and batch production

In this chapter you will:
★ learn about **one-off** and **batch production** of food products.

One-off production

One-off production

One-off production is when one food product is made at a time or on demand. This is the type of production you usually carry out in the classroom or at home.

When a chef produces products for a celebration buffet, he or she is carrying out one-off production. He or she uses his skill and spends a long time creating the buffet.

Batch production

Batch production is repetitive, small-scale manufacture of the same product by a team. The same equipment is used to make a variety of products, such as different kinds of cakes or bread, or even different flavoured sausages.

Country Cakes

Country Cakes Ltd is based in the village of Knowle Green in Lancashire. There are six employees, working full-time and part-time, who help to produce about 2000 cakes a week.

The ingredients are bought in bulk (photo A). This means they are about 25% cheaper than supermarket prices.

A

B

Large quantities of cake mixture are made at a time in a big food mixer that is so big it has to be on the floor (photo B).

Mr Yates, the boss, uses a ladle to pour the mixture into cake tins (photo C). They have the same quantity of mixture in each tin. This is because Mr Yates is skilled in getting the same amount into each tin. He has had a lot of experience. If a less experienced worker did this job, they could use weighing scales to check that the cakes weigh the same.

The cakes are baked in a deck oven (photo D) with ten deep shelves above each other. This means that a lot of products can be baked at the same time but at different temperatures. A timer is used so that the cakes do not overcook.

C

D

When the cooked cakes have cooled a little, they are manually lifted out of the tins (photo E) and put onto cooling racks.

Most of the cakes are iced or have a layer of jam (photo F). Mrs Yates spoons the same amount of icing or jam onto each cake and spreads it quickly over the top. Mrs Yates is also skilled at her job – she knows how much to put onto the cake and how to spread it smoothly. She must not lift her palette knife off the icing as this will cause the top of the cake to break up.

E

F

The cakes are delivered all over north-west England to supermarkets and other retail shops such as newsagents and garages. They are also delivered to tourist attractions where they are served in cafés.

I

Most of the cakes are sold as individual portions. One of the part-time workers cuts the cakes with either an ordinary knife or an electric hand-knife (photo G). This is time-consuming but, as this is a batch production operation, it was decided that an expensive machine that cuts cakes using a laser was too expensive.

The cakes are packed in cellophane and sealed (photo H). A simple label, which has been designed and printed using a DTP program on an ordinary computer, is stuck onto each cake portion (photo I). This gives information on what it is, the ingredients, who has made it and when it should be eaten by.

G

H

Coursework

You will need to consider how your product could be produced as one-offs or in batches. Use the information in this chapter to help you to consider industrial practices, systems and controls. Could your product be batch produced? If so, how?

Activity

Draw a flow chart to show the batch production of cakes at Country Cakes. Show which tasks are done manually and which are done by machines. Include the kind of controls and **feedback** that would be included in the **system**.

Summary

★ One-off production is when one special product is made.

★ Nearly all the food products produced for other people are batch or mass produced.

★ Batch production is relatively small-scale. A mixture of skilled workers and machines is used.

Making food products commercially

Mass and other methods of production

<table>
<tr><td>

In this chapter you will:
* ★ learn about the **mass production** of food products.

</td></tr>
</table>

Mass production

This is large-scale manufacturing on a production line where most of the processes are carried out by computerised machines – **computer-aided manufacture (CAM)**. Mass production can be continuous, where a production line runs uninterrupted twenty-four hours a day, seven days a week (except for cleaning), because it is run by computers and machines rather than people. Thousands of the same products are made at a time. The production line is a continuously moving conveyor belt.

Other production methods

Continuous flow production is when there is a production line or whole factory that is dedicated to one product. The only time the production line is stopped is for cleaning and maintenance of the machinery. There has to be a high demand for these products for them to be made continuously. One example is potato crisps. The different flavourings are added at the end of the process, which means there is just one production line to clean and peel the potatoes, slice them and then cook them.

Just-in-time production is another method used by some food manufacturers so that they do not have to store large quantities of ingredients. These ingredients are delivered several times during the day, just in time to be used in the process.

Computerised equipment

Mass production is computer-aided manufacture. Computerised equipment carries out the processes. Some of this equipment is similar to items used at home or at school, such as electrical mixers, electronic scales and boiling vats, but many pieces of equipment are computer controlled. Other items are specialised pieces that you will not have seen before such as depositors and shapers.

Case Study

McVities

McVities is a mass-producer of biscuits such as the McVities Chocolate Digestive. Over 71 million packets (52 biscuits per second) of this biscuit are eaten each year in the UK.

The factory has several production lines. Each production line makes the same biscuit every day. The digestive biscuit line produces thousands of biscuits a minute.

Very large quantities of ingredients are used. These are delivered in tankers (photo A) and piped into large storage containers.

A

When these ingredients are needed, they are piped into a large mixing machine (photo B). A computer measures the correct amount of each ingredient (photo C). The machine is programmed to mix the biscuit mixture for the right length of time and at the correct speed.

B

The mixture is then poured into a computerised depositor that pushes it through roller moulds to shape the biscuits at a programmed rate and speed (photo D).

C

D

This is where the conveyor belt starts. The biscuits are dropped onto this production line – the speed is controlled by computer so that when the biscuits go through the tunnel oven (photo E) they are cooked correctly.

E

This tunnel oven is set at different temperatures for the different stages of baking. This could not be done in an ordinary oven unless you manually changed the temperature halfway through baking the biscuits. This oven is also computer controlled. If temperatures drop below a certain level, an alarm alerts the workers.

When the cooked biscuits come out of the tunnel oven, they go into the computer-controlled cooling tower where they go round and round on the conveyor belt to cool them down. Some digestive biscuits then get coated with chocolate (photo F).

F

Computerised machines group the biscuits before wrapping them in packaging (photo G).

G

This is the end of the conveyor belt. Workers put the packets of biscuits into boxes ready to be transported all over the UK (photos H and I).

H

I

Coursework

You will need to consider how your product could be mass produced. Use the information in this chapter to help you to consider industrial practices, systems and controls. Could your product be mass produced? If so, how?

Activity

Draw a flow chart to show the mass production of biscuits at McVities. Show which tasks are controlled by computer. Include the kind of controls and **feedback** that would be included in the **system**.

Summary

★ Mass production is when computerised equipment carries out the process so that hundreds of the same food product can be made very quickly.

Making food products commercially

Health and safety controls

In this chapter you will:

★ learn about the importance of health and safety controls.

When you make a food product, you have to make sure it is safe to eat as well as of good quality. You do this by applying good health and safety controls, which are part of the **quality control system**.

You carry out basic health and safety controls when you make a food product at home or in the classroom so that you do not cause food poisoning. For example, you:

- wash your hands
- wear an apron
- tie back long hair
- use clean equipment and surfaces
- store some foods in the fridge.

When food is made for other people, health and safety controls become even more important because of the health risks to many people. Workers can be prosecuted (they are personally liable) if they cause illness, so they must make sure they follow strict health and safety controls.

Personal hygiene

Washing hands carefully is vital. Many people do not clean around the thumbs, between the fingers, and around and under the nails. Hands should be rubbed vigorously for fifteen seconds. In food production, soap is used before an alcoholic wash. There are no hand taps – water is turned on by the knee. Hands have to be washed every time you:

- go to the toilet
- blow your nose
- have a break
- work with raw ingredients, particularly **high-risk foods** such as meat, fish and dairy products
- move to a different production area, for example start to work with cooked food
- cough, or touch your face or hair.

Equipment and cleaning

In a food factory, cleaning control systems are in place so that workers know that the equipment they use is safe to use – clean from dirt and contamination.

What needs to be cleaned at least once a day?

- All food contact surfaces – all equipment including knives, chopping boards and work surfaces.
- All hand contact surfaces – handles, taps and switches and anything the hand touches.
- Special **hazard** areas like waste bins, cloths and mops.

Food workers wear more than just an apron.

Food workers must:

wear clean overalls that cover all their ordinary clothing

wear at least one hair net (most wear two), as up to 100 hairs are lost each day

wear special footwear, such as Wellingtons, which are not used outside the production area so that bacteria from outside is not carried in

wear gloves to work in or wash their hands properly, as hands are in most contact with food

not wear make-up, perfume, aftershave and jewellery as these can contaminate food

cover cuts with blue plasters as these are easily seen if they fall off and report any illnesses they are suffering

not cough, sneeze or spit over food as this spreads bacteria

not pick their noses or lick food

How should they be cleaned?

Washing-up liquid is a detergent that helps to dissolve grease and remove dirt. It does not remove bacteria. Equipment should be disinfected so that bacteria are reduced to a low, safe level. Disinfection can be achieved by the use of:

- very hot water – at least 82°C or hotter
- steam
- chemical disinfectants.

Hand-hot water will kill some bacteria, although people can only withstand temperatures of no more than 40°C. Therefore, hot water should be combined with the use of a disinfectant. A sanitiser is a detergent and disinfectant combined, so it does two jobs at the same time.

WASH WITH HOT WATER AND SANITISER

LEAVE ENOUGH TIME FOR SANITISER TO KILL ANY BACTERIA.

RINSE OFF WITH CLEAN HOT WATER

Sanitisers are detergents and disinfectants combined

The other important thing to consider when cleaning equipment is the cloths, sponges and tea towels that are used. How clean are they? Different cloths should be used for different tasks, and tea towels should be used as little as possible. It is better to leave equipment to dry and to dry hands on paper towels.

In a food factory, there should be clear, detailed cleaning schedules so that equipment is cleaned properly to prevent the risk of food poisoning.

Coursework

Health and safety controls have to be considered during all making activities so that you show you have worked safely and that you have considered quality controls.

Activities

1 Make a list of the main points you would make to a new food worker when they:
   a arrive at work
   b dress for work
   c wash their hands.

2 Look at the following list of equipment and work areas. Explain which items you think need to be cleaned monthly, weekly, daily or after every task. Explain your answers.
   - Taps on handbasins.
   - Walls.
   - Floors in food preparation areas.
   - A slicing machine.
   - Fridge or cupboard handles.
   - Food utensils such as knives and spoons.
   - Floors in dry store area.

3 Design a poster for a commercial food production company to raise awareness of how to handle and store food properly.

Summary

★ Good personal hygiene and the correct cleaning of equipment are essential health and safety controls when making food products.

Making food products commercially

4.5 Bacteria and temperature controls

In this chapter you will:

★ learn more about bacteria so that you understand the importance of temperature control, especially with **high-risk foods**.

An outbreak of E.coli in Lanarkshire, Scotland affected 400 people and caused 18 deaths. The outbreak was caused by poor hygiene practices that allowed **cross-contamination** from raw meat to cooked meat products.

Bacteria can make you ill by causing food poisoning.
- Food poisoning is very unpleasant. It causes diarrhoea, vomiting, stomach cramps and fever.
- It is potentially serious as shown in the newspaper article above. The young, the old, pregnant and nursing mothers, and those who are already unwell are the most vulnerable.
- It can be prevented through good hygiene practices.

'Good' bacteria

Some forms of bacteria can be good for us. We have 'good' bacteria in our digestive systems, which help break down certain foods. We add 'good' bacteria to some yoghurt, cheeses and drinks.

'Bad' bacteria

These are the bacteria we must be concerned about. There are two kinds of bad bacteria:
- spoilage bacteria, which make food go bad
- pathogenic bacteria, which cause food poisoning or food-borne disease.

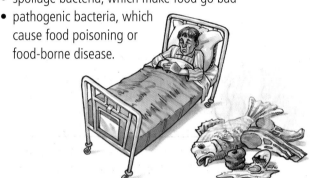

The two kinds of bad bacteria

	Sources	Symptoms
Pathogenic bacteria		
Salmonella	Raw poultry, eggs, raw meat, milk, animals (including pets), insects and sewage	Onset 12–36 hours; abdominal pain, diarrhoea, vomiting, fever
Stapphylococcus aureus	The human body, especially skin, nose, mouth, cuts and boils, and raw milk	Onset 1–6 hours; abdominal pain or cramps, vomiting, low temperature
Clostridium perfigens	Animal and human excreta, soil, dust, insects and raw meat	Onset 12–18 hours; abdominal pain, diarrhoea
Bacillus cereus	Cereals, especially rice; some are resistant to heat	Onset 1–16 hours; abdominal pain, some diarrhoea, vomiting
Clostridium botulinum	Canned fish, meat and vegetables, soil, smoked fish	Onset 12–36 hours; difficulties in breathing and swallowing, blurred vision; death in a week or slow recovery over months
Food-borne illnesses		
E.coli	Human and animal gut, which can be transferred to the meat during slaughter, sewage, water, raw meat	Onset 12–24 hours; abdominal pain, fever, diarrhoea, vomiting, kidney damage or failure
Campylobacter	Meat and poultry, milk and animals	Onset 48–60 hours; diarrhoea (often bloody), abdominal pain, nausea, fever
Listeria	Grows at low temperatures in a fridge. Soft cheese, cheese made from unpasteurised milk, paté, salad, vegetables	Onset 1–70 days; flu-type symptoms; meningitis-like symptoms

Different bacteria cause different symptoms

The types of bacteria that cause food poisoning come from five main sources:

- raw foods, especially meat, poultry, eggs, shellfish and vegetables
- pets and pests such as rats, mice and insects
- people, from skin, noses, mouths, ears, hair and sometimes the gut
- air and dust
- food waste and rubbish.

Examples of pathogenic bacteria and food-borne illnesses are shown in the table opposite.

How bacteria multiply

Bacteria reproduce rapidly by dividing in two. This means that two becomes four, four becomes eight and so on. Each bacterium needs between 10 and 20 minutes to multiply in ideal conditions. You can work out how quickly one bacterium becomes millions. For example, two bacteria on a sausage left out in a kitchen overnight could have multiplied to around 500 million bacteria by the time you come to eat it for breakfast.

Ideal conditions

Bacteria have four main requirements.

- **Food:** bacteria prefer foods that are moist and high in protein. Such foods include meat, poultry, fish, eggs, and dairy products. These are called high-risk foods. Particular

care must be taken when working with these foods so there is no cross-contamination between raw and cooked foods (or foods that are eaten raw such as salad and vegetables).

- **Moisture:** bacteria need moisture to stay alive. They cannot multiply in dried foods. However, as soon as liquid is added to foods such as gravy or custard powder, they become ideal conditions for bacteria.
- **Warmth:** most bacteria multiply above 5°C and below 63°C. Any temperature in this range is called the **danger zone**. High-risk foods are kept below 5°C (in a fridge) or cooked above 63°C. It is recommended that the core temperature in the centre of the food is above 72°C for at least two minutes. Frozen foods are kept at −18°C, which slows bacteria growth.
- **Time:** bacteria multiply quickly. The first 60–90 minutes is OK, while the food is cooling down, but after that multiplication gets serious! It is recommended that food should be chilled to below 5°C within 90 minutes if it is to be stored.

If you know the conditions that bacteria need to grow, you can carry out health and safety controls to stop this growth. You need to be particularly careful with high-risk foods to avoid cross-contamination. You can carry out temperature controls by making sure you store all high-risk food below 5°C and cook it to above 72°C. Use a temperature probe to check these temperatures.

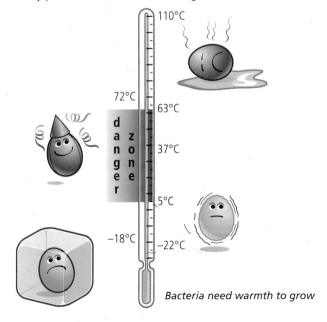

Bacteria need warmth to grow

Activity

Imagine you work for a catering company that has been asked to produce a buffet for a party. Three of the foods to be served are prawn cocktail, chicken kiev and chocolate mousse. Explain the important hygiene controls you will carry out, including time and temperature controls, to make sure the food will be safe to eat.

Summary

★ Cold food must be stored at 0–5°C.

★ Cooked food, particularly high-risk food, must reach a core temperature of 72°C for two minutes and not cool down below 63°C.

★ Bacteria do not die when chilled or frozen.

Making food products commercially

In this chapter you will:
★ learn about **risk assessment** and **HACCP**.

Health and safety controls are extremely important in the food industry. Food products must be safe to eat. Food manufacturers must show **due diligence** when they produce and store food products. This means they must have thought about and done everything possible to make sure they are producing safe food products. Environmental health officers have the power to fine a business or close it down if their hygiene controls are not of an acceptable standard. Food manufacturers can end up in prison and paying compensation to customers.

Therefore, food manufacturers must make sure:

* the premises are registered and they are designed, equipped and operated in ways that prevent contamination and anything that could lead to illness or injury
* staff are trained and supervised to work hygienically and that there are adequate washing facilities and arrangements for personal hygiene
* food **hazards** are assessed and action taken to stop or reduce risks to food safety – this is known as risk assessment or hazard analysis.

Hazards

In food products, a hazard is anything that is likely to cause harm to a customer. There are three kinds of hazards:

* biological: bacterial contamination or the possibility of bacterial contamination caused by pathogenic bacteria (food-poisoning bacteria)
* chemical: food being contaminated by cleaning fluids during processing or storage. Chemical contamination could mean that ingredients are affected by pesticides or pest bait, or contaminated by oil or paint on machinery
* physical: this could be stones, pips, leaves or stalks from fruit and vegetables; shell fragments from nuts, eggs or shellfish; paper string, plastic or staples from food packaging; nuts, bolts and screws from machinery; jewellery, hair, fingernails, buttons, pen tops and plasters; insects and other similar creatures.

All sorts of hazards exist, which could harm people when they eat the food

Risks

In food production, a risk is the likelihood of a hazard happening. For example, if you use a sieve in the process that flour has to pass through, what is the likelihood of the food being contaminated with stones? If you check the temperature of the meat on delivery, what is the likelihood of bacterial growth on the meat?

Risk assessment

Risk assessment is thinking about what could happen, when it could happen, and taking steps to prevent it happening. Hazard analysis is the same thing; analysis means looking in detail at something and working out what, when and how the hazard could happen.

HACCP

The food industry uses a risk assessment system called **Hazard Analysis Critical Control Points (HACCP)** so that quality products are produced. This system identifies hazards and analyses them at certain stages called **critical control points (CCP)** to see if they are high risk (critical). It then works out what control would reduce the risk of the hazard happening. If this system is used, every product would be produced safely and would not be a risk to the customer.

equipment

food product

Where do possible hazards come from?

enviroment

production process

workers

Many food manufacturers use **computer-aided design (CAD)** and **computer-aided manufacture (CAM)** to help them with their HACCP system. Specialist computer programs help manufacturers identify possible hazards. Computerised equipment helps with temperature control. For example, hand-held temperature probes are linked to a computer that logs the temperature without the worker having to write down the temperature manually.

How does HACCP work?

The HACCP procedure seems complicated at first, but if it is carried out in a systematic way, it can be straightforward. Here are the stages in the system.

1 Write down each stage in the production **system**.
2 Work out if there is a possible hazard at this stage.
3 Explain why this hazard is a risk.
4 Work out a control check to stop the hazard or reduce the likelihood of it happening.
5 Work out the action you would take if the control shows the hazard has happened.

The table gives an example for a chicken and vegetable curry.

Coursework

When writing a manufacturing **specification**, you will need to consider health and safety controls. The best way to do this is to carry out a risk assessment and then write a HACCP plan.

Activity

Identify the hazards during the production of a batch of chicken pies. Work out the controls you would put in place to stop these hazards taking place.

Summary

★ Risk assessment and HACCP are an important part of **quality assurance** in the food industry.

Stage in production system	Risk/hazard	Reasons why it is a risk	Symptoms	Action to take if control shows risk has happened
Delivery of goods	Damaged Out of date Wrong temperature	All make food unsafe to eat	Visual check Visual check Use temperature probe for correct temperature	Reject Reject Reject
Wash vegetables properly	Contamination from dirt/chemicals	Makes food unsafe to eat	Thorough cleaning	Clean again and recheck
Dice chicken fillets evenly	Salmonella from uneven cooking	Salmonella lives in poultry and causes food poisoning. Uneven cooking increases the risk of salmonella not being killed during cooking	Use temperature probe to check temperature of chicken is below 5°C Visual check for size	Reject Train staff
Cook chicken pieces thoroughly	Salmonella from inadequate cooking	Salmonella causes food poisoning	Use temperature probe to check temperature of chicken is 70°C for two minutes	Cook longer

Making food products commercially

In this chapter you will:

★ learn how important it is to make sure food product quality is controlled and that products are the same each time they are made.

When you make a food product at home or in the classroom, you automatically use **quality controls** so that you produce an acceptable product. Those used when making bread are given on page 56. If something goes wrong, such as the lid falling off when you were pouring some salt in to flavour the bread, you might throw the bread away and start again – or you might try to eat it!

Accidents like this need to be avoided when making food for other people

When food is made for other people, mistakes like the one above cannot be allowed to happen. You would lose money and customers. The food production **system** has to be set up with quality controls in place so that the right quality product is manufactured again and again. If you are a food manufacturer, you have to guarantee the quality of your food. **Consumers** expect the same quality of product every time they buy and eat it.

Quality means 'a certain standard', so with food production this means that the:

- ingredients of the food product will be the same – the manufacturer will not suddenly decide to change the ingredients

- way the product is made will stay the same, for example the manufacturer will not suddenly decide to cook the dish for twice as long.

Quality control

Quality control means to check the standards of a food product as it is being designed and made. When the product is being designed, it will be checked to see if it matches the outline **specification**.

Does the product match the outline specification?

When the product is being manufactured, many quality control checks will be carried out:

- visual checks: are the raw ingredients the right size and colour? Has the machine shaped the biscuits correctly?
- physical contamination checks: a metal detector is often used at the packaging stage

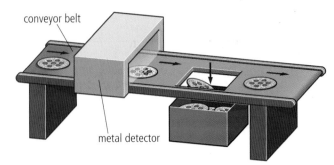

- weight checks: is the depositor putting enough tomato sauce onto the bases?

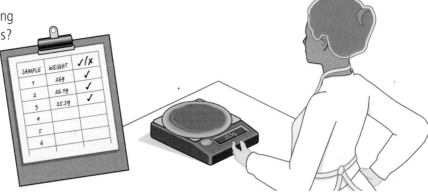

SAMPLE	WEIGHT	✓/✗
1	26g	✓
2	26.1g	✓
3	25.5g	✓
4		
5		
6		

- time checks: is the speed of the conveyor belt allowing the biscuits enough time in the cooling towers?
- temperature checks: is the temperature of the freezer being kept below −18°C?
- biological and chemical contamination checks: samples are tested to ensure they are free from bacteria and chemicals.

If **CAM** is used, some of these checks become easier because they are computer controlled.

Once the product has been manufactured, it will be checked regularly to make sure it is always of the same standard and quality. All food manufacturers have daily (or twice daily) tasting sessions where the taste, texture, appearance and size or shape is checked against the specification. These are **organoleptic** (sensory) checks.

Some checks must be precise, but others can just be within a **tolerance**. Contamination and temperature checks must be precise – they must meet a precise standard or the food will be unsafe to eat. Organoleptic (including visual) and weight checks do not have to be quite so precise. For example, the weight of a finished pizza must be between 175 and 185 grams. The colour of a burger bun must be no lighter than a certain brown and no darker than another brown. These checks are to make sure the product is within a designated tolerance.

So, you can see that food manufacturers do a lot to make sure they produce quality products. Quality means repeat sales and increased sales – it means making a **profit**. Poor quality means the opposite.

Quality assurance

Quality assurance is a system used by food manufacturers to describe and guarantee the total standard of the food products they produce. It means a guarantee of quality. Quality controls are part of quality assurance. Other things covered by quality assurance are:

- packaging
- distribution and selling of the product
- what ingredients are used
- what the food product is like
- how the product is made
- how the workforce is trained
- the hygiene procedures that are being followed.

Coursework

You will need to provide evidence that you have considered and applied quality controls and quality assurance.

Test your knowledge

1 What does 'quality' mean?
2 What does 'quality control' mean?
3 List all the different quality controls that can be carried out.

Summary

★ Food manufacturers have to follow a quality assurance system that includes good quality controls if they want to stay in business.

Making food products commercially

4.8 Quality controls in the classroom

In this chapter you will:

★ learn how to use the examples of **quality controls** used in food manufacturing to make better quality food products in the classroom.

You have learnt how important it is that the quality of manufactured food products stays the same every time they are made. Quality control checks are carried out all the time. These are:

- weight and size controls
- temperature controls
- time controls
- visual controls
- **organoleptic** (sensory) controls
- hygiene (biological, physical and chemical) controls.

CAM and quality controls

When food products are mass produced, computers can be used to control the process. Food manufacturers use **CAM** to produce and help control the quality of products.

- Sensors are used to monitor some processes such as oven temperature, pH of a mixture like yoghurt, and the weight of component parts or final product. Computers provide instant **feedback** to the **system** so that parts can be altered if needed.
- Detection systems, such as a metal detectors, can be used towards the end of the process, or detectors that identify micro-organisms can be used.
- Robotics are used for tasks that require repetitive actions, especially on production lines that run 24 hours a day. A robot can be programmed to pipe an exact amount of mashed potato on top of a shepherd's pie, for example. A series of robots can make sandwiches, including adding a small amount of cress to the filling. They can be used for repetitive, heavy and unpleasant tasks.
- Stock control: computers can be used to forecast demand and sales, and stock control. Christmas might influence the demand of some products, and warm weather others.

- Digital imaging is used to monitor the size, shape and position of some ingredients. Digital images can be sent to the computer so changes to the system can be instant.
- Sensory analysis: results can be input into a computer so that data can be instantly and easily analysed.

Understanding quality controls

Computer-aided controls are not easy to use in the classroom, but they can be useful in helping you to understand quality controls. They make it easier for you to identify:

- where you need to control
- what kind of control you could use.

Robots can be used in food manufacture

If you use the list of controls at the top of the opposite page as a check, you can identify ways that using controls will help you in the classroom:
- use reliable scales, preferably electronic
- use cutters and shapers for equal sizes, such as rolling guides to control the thickness of pastry and biscuits, burger makers, biscuit cutters, ravioli rollers, ice cream scoops

Using the right equipment will help with your quality controls

- use thermometers inside ovens, fridges and freezers to check temperatures and when making bread, yoghurt or cheese
- check the colour of your cake against the **specification**: use paint charts to identify your desired colour of golden brown
- carry out sensory analysis of your product. Record your results so that you can use them to make a quality product again or to make improvements
- carry out a **risk assessment** so that you make a food product that is safe to eat. Use your knowledge of health and safety, temperature controls, **high-risk foods**, storage and cleaning to work out how to be safe.

You can also use quality controls before you start to make a product. When you purchase the ingredients, you decide on the quality of ingredient you will use.
- How much money will I spend on the sausagemeat for my sausage rolls? How much fat will be in the meat?
- Do I want ready-grated cheese, or do I want to grate it myself? Maybe I should buy a block of cheese.
- Shall I use a pastry mix to save time or do I want to decide on the kind of fat that will be in my pastry so make it from scratch?

Coursework

Although you will not be able to carry out all these quality controls the same way as a food manufacturer, you should show that during designing and making you have used quality controls to produce accurate and consistent final products.

Activity

Make a list of the quality controls that can be used to produce a batch of lamb samosas.

Summary

★ Using quality controls during the input, process and output of a food **system** – including a **one-off production** in the classroom – will ensure that a quality product will be made.

Making food products commercially

Standard components

In this chapter you will:
★ learn how and when to use standard components in food production.

Using standard food components is one way of controlling the quality of a product. You will use standard (ready-made) components when you make food products at home or in school. Food manufacturers also use standard food products.

For example, if you were asked to produce twenty strawberry tarts for a special lunch, you could make the shortcrust pastry yourself and wash, slice and cook fresh strawberries for the filling. Alternatively, you could use some standard components instead.

Which method would you choose and why? Here are some of the advantages and disadvantages of both methods.

Handmade method

Handmade

Pastry: 200 g plain flour
100 g butter
50 g caster sugar
Water

Filling: 500 g strawberries
150 g caster sugar
50 g cornflour
Water

Advantages

You will be able to make the quality of pastry you want. You could add sugar or an egg to make a rich pastry. You could choose the quality of strawberries and the amount of sugar you add to them.

Disadvantages

If you were making these tarts in winter, fresh strawberries would be expensive to use as they would not be in season in the UK and would have to be imported from abroad. It will take you some time to make the pastry, the filling and then assemble the tarts. You need to be skilled in pastry making and know how to control the cooking and thickening of the strawberry filling. You need to be able to store the fat and strawberries in a fridge to keep them fresh. You need to be skilled in rolling out pastry.

Standard components method

Standard components

Pastry: 500 g short crust pastry mix
Packet of ready-rolled pastry circles

Filling: 750 g tinned strawberry pie filling

Advantages

You do not need to be skilled in pastry making and will have no preparation or cooking for the filling. If you use ready-rolled pastry, you will only have to assemble the pies.

It will not take much time to make them. The strawberry pie filling could be cheaper to buy than fresh strawberries if strawberries were not in season.

Disadvantages

A pastry mix or ready-rolled pastry is more expensive to buy than the raw ingredients if you were to make pastry from scratch. You will have no control over the nutritional content of the components such as how much fat is in the pastry, what kind of fat is used, and how much sugar is in the filling. You will also have no control over ingredients added to these components such as colourings and preservatives. You will have to accept the quality of these products.

Other standard components

Other examples of standard components include:
• stock cubes

Ready-grated cheese is a standard component

- chopped dried herbs
- grated cheese
- cake mixes
- pizza bases.

Activities

1 a Write a list of standard components that you could use for a chilli con carne, and syrup sponge and custard.
   b Compare the cost of using standard components and the cost of buying all raw ingredients for these two dishes.

2 a Make two different pizzas: one using a ready-made pizza base, a ready-made tomato sauce and pre-grated cheese, the other using bread dough, a homemade tomato sauce and a block of cheese you grate yourself. Complete a sensory comparison of the two pizzas.
   b Use nutritional analysis to see if there is a difference in nutritional content.

Summary

★ Standard components control the quality of food products so that they always look and taste the same.

★ There are some disadvantages to using standard components.

Case Study

Pizzas made from standard components

A pizza factory that mass produces thousands of pizzas a day uses ready-diced cheese. Other ready-made components it uses are ready-sliced packets of mixed colour peppers and mushrooms, ready-diced and cooked chicken and ham pieces, and ready-washed and chopped herbs. The ready-sliced peppers would match the **specification** set by the company, for example each slice will be the right width and length. These components would be checked on delivery against the specification.

Making food products commercially

Uses of packaging and labelling

Nearly all the food we buy today is packaged. Billions of pounds are spent every year on packaging food products.

In the past, food was measured out for each individual customer. Tea leaves were weighed into paper bags, a piece of cheese was cut off a block and wrapped in waxed paper, even milk used to be measured into a jug the customer brought out to the delivery cart.

Years ago, food products were measured out for each customer

Today, self-service shopping means most foods need to be pre-packaged. The reasons foods are packaged include:
* protection from physical damage during transportation and storage such as eggs in an egg box. Some foods are contained by the packaging such as soups and other liquid foods
* protection from bacterial damage, moisture or insect attack. Some packaging, such as tins, preserves food for a long time
* to prevent tampering by other people
* to provide customers with information on how to store and cook the food, and what ingredients are in it
* to attract customers in advertising the product
* to use when the food is reheated.

When food manufacturers are designing packaging, they have to consider three main points: the design, the information needed and the materials to use. We will look at the design and the information in this chapter, and packaging materials in chapter 4.11.

The design

The design of the package is usually done by a design (graphics) company. This specialist company will consider the colours, font type and size to use. It will also arrange for a specialist photographer to produce a photo of the product so that the initial impact of the packaging is appealing to the customer.

Part of the manufacturing **specification** (see page 83) includes information about the packaging:
* the information required by law, including storage conditions and **shelf life**
* allergen information, such as whether the product contains nuts or eggs, for those who are allergic to certain ingredients
* inner product packaging such as description, materials used and dimensions
* outer product packaging (usually paperboard sleeve or box) such as description, materials used and dimensions.

The information needed

The law says that some information has to be included on all food packaging. It is compulsory to provide the following information:
* the name of the food
* a description of the product (this can be a basic one or use adjectives, such as rich, succulent or creamy, to help sell the product)
* the name and address of the manufacturer or seller
* storage instructions
* cooking or preparation instructions
* weight or volume
* a list of ingredients (the heaviest first)
* the 'use by' date.

Some food manufacturers also include some of the following information on their packaging:
* bar or smart codes: nearly all packaging has one of these. They identify the price and are used by shops and manufacturers for stock control
* nutritional information: most food products include basic

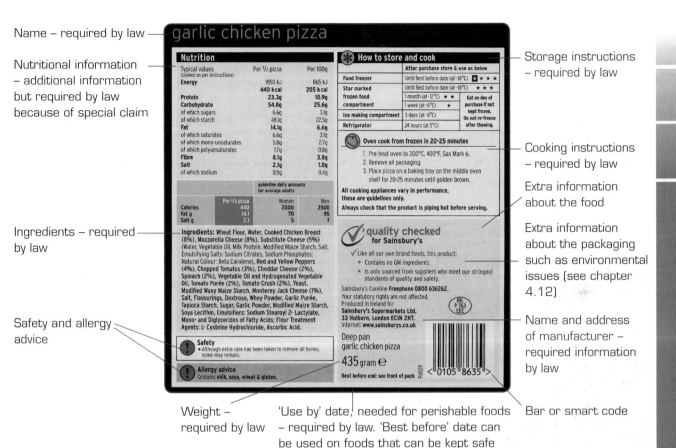

Name – required by law

Nutritional information – additional information but required by law because of special claim

Ingredients – required by law

Safety and allergy advice

garlic chicken pizza

Nutrition

Typical values (cooked as per instructions)	Per ½ pizza	Per 100g
Energy	1850 kJ	865 kJ
	440 kcal	205 kcal
Protein	23.3g	10.9g
Carbohydrate	54.8g	25.6g
of which sugars	6.6g	3.1g
of which starch	48.1g	22.5g
Fat	14.1g	6.6g
of which saturates	6.6g	3.1g
of which mono-unsaturates	5.8g	2.7g
of which polyunsaturates	1.7g	0.8g
Fibre	8.1g	3.8g
Salt	2.1g	1.0g
of which sodium	0.9g	0.4g

guideline daily amounts for average adults			
	Per ½ pizza	Women	Men
Calories	440	2000	2500
Fat g	14.1	70	95
Salt g	2.1	5	7

Ingredients: Wheat Flour, Water, Cooked Chicken Breast (8%), Mozzarella Cheese (8%), Substitute Cheese (5%) (Water, Vegetable Oil, Milk Protein, Modified Maize Starch, Salt, Emulsifying Salts: Sodium Citrates, Sodium Phosphates; Natural Colour: Beta Carotene), Red and Yellow Peppers (4%), Chopped Tomatos (3%), Cheddar Cheese (2%), Spinach (2%), Vegetable Oil and Hydrogenated Vegetable Oil, Tomato Purée (2%), Tomato Crush (2%), Yeast, Modified Waxy Maize Starch, Monterey Jack Cheese (1%), Salt, Flavourings, Dextrose, Whey Powder, Garlic Purée, Tapioca Starch, Sugar, Garlic Powder, Modified Maize Starch, Soya Lecithin, Emulsifiers: Sodium Stearoyl 2- Lactylate, Mono- and Diglycerides of Fatty Acids; Flour Treatment Agents: L- Cysteine Hydrochloride, Ascorbic Acid.

(!) Safety
• Although extra care has been taken to remove all bones, some may remain.

(!) Allergy advice
Contains milk, soya, wheat & gluten.

❄ How to store and cook

	After purchase store & use as below
Food freezer	Until Best before date (at -18°C) ✱ ★ ★ ★
Star marked frozen food compartment	Until Best before date (at -18°C) ★ ★ ★
	1 month (at -12°C) ★ ★ · Eat on day of purchase if not kept frozen. Do not re-freeze after thawing.
	1 week (at -6°C) ★
Ice making compartment	3 days (at -6°C)
Refrigerator	24 hours (at 5°C)

Oven cook from frozen in 20-25 minutes

1. Pre-heat oven to 200°C, 400°F, Gas Mark 6.
2. Remove all packaging.
3. Place pizza on a baking tray on the middle oven shelf for 20-25 minutes until golden brown.

All cooking appliances vary in performance, these are guidelines only.
Always check that the product is piping hot before serving.

✓ quality checked for Sainsbury's

✓ Like all our own brand foods, this product:
• Contains no GM ingredients.
• Is only sourced from suppliers who meet our stringent standards of quality and safety.

Sainsbury's Careline Freephone 0800 636262.
Your statutory rights are not affected.
Produced in Ireland for
Sainsbury's Supermarkets Ltd,
33 Holborn, London ECIN 2HT.
Internet: www.sainsburys.co.uk

Deep pan
garlic chicken pizza

435 gram ℮

Best before end: see front of pack

IRL P 763 EEC

0105 8635

Storage instructions – required by law

Cooking instructions – required by law

Extra information about the food

Extra information about the packaging such as environmental issues (see chapter 4.12)

Name and address of manufacturer – required information by law

Weight – required by law

'Use by' date, needed for perishable foods – required by law. 'Best before' date can be used on foods that can be kept safe for a long time such as tinned foods

Bar or smart code

Packaging may contain detailed information about the product

nutritional information. If the special claim is about a nutrient, this information must be included
• the price, although lots of packaging do not show a price as the bar code identifies this
• serving suggestions such as serve with custard or cream
• more information about the ingredients such as what is not contained in the product like gluten or dairy produce
• recycling logos and anti-litter symbols to encourage **consumers** to recycle
• any other information or special claims such as low fat.

🔘 **Coursework**

You need to consider what information will be on the packaging of your final food product, but you will not need to design and make it.

✏ Activities

1 What are the different purposes of packaging?
2 Is it a good idea for food manufacturers to include extra information on their packaging such as serving suggestions and more information about the ingredients?

Summary

★ Packaging has many uses.

★ Three things have to be considered when designing packaging: the design, the information needed and the materials to be used.

★ Labelling is important because it provides lots of information about the product.

Making food products commercially

4.11 Selecting suitable packaging materials

In this chapter you will:

★ find out what packaging materials are best for different food products.

This product has paperboard packaging

Recycled paperboard is used for the outer packaging of this product. The food is contained in a microwaveable and ovenable thermoplastic (polyester PET) for the base and film. Other materials, such as aluminium foil or ovenable paperboard, could have been used.

Packaging choices

The choice of packaging depends on the food it will contain, how long it will be kept in the packaging and what will be done with the food once it is opened. Will it be eaten cold from the packet? Cooked first? You need to look at the product **specification** to decide what packaging would be most suitable.

Materials used in packaging

Thermoplastics

There are many types of plastic, each with their own characteristics. They all have the same general advantages:
- they are lightweight
- cheap to produce

- flexible or rigid (depending on the type of plastic)
- water resistant
- resistant to acids/chemicals
- easily printed on
- good food protectors
- heat resistant if necessary.

The main disadvantages are:
- many **consumers** do not recycle these items
- the use of thermoplastics is not sustainable as they are made from non-renewable resources.

Thermoplastics are suitable for a range of food products.

Metal

Steel and aluminium are both used in food packaging and are suitable for liquids.

The advantages of steel are:
- it can be recycled and reclaimed easily (using a magnet)
- it is strong
- it extends the **shelf life** of food it contains (canning).

The disadvantages of steel are:
- it cannot be used in microwaves
- it can react with some foods so that some cans need a non-metallic lining.

Steel is suitable for long-term packaging, such as canned foods.

The advantages of aluminium are:
- it is pliable
- it is opened easily with ring pulls
- it can be made into different shapes
- it can be recycled easily.

The disadvantage is that aluminium cannot be used in a microwave.

Glass

Glass has many advantages:
- it is cheap to produce
- you can see the food through it
- it is rigid (keeps its shape)
- it can withstand heat
- it can be recycled
- it can be resealed easily.

The main disadvantages to glass are
• its weight
• how easily it breaks.

Glass is suitable for products such as pickles, where the packaging can also be reused.

Paper and paperboard

The advantages of paper are:
• it can be printed on easily
• it is cheap to make
• it is biodegradable, recyclable and comes from a sustainable resource
• it can be shaped easily
• it can be made in different thicknesses
• if it is corrugated, it protects and insulates the product.

The disadvantages of paper are:
• it can be squashed easily
• it is not water resistant unless it is coated with wax or plastic.

Paper and paperboard are suitable for outer packaging and for dry products such as teabags.

Matching packaging to purpose

Different packaging materials are right for different products. For example, pickled onions might need a glass jar, teabags a paperboard box and meat a water-resistant plastic container. However, some packaging materials are a combination of several materials:

• **ovenable paperboard** has a coating of polyester PET so that it can withstand temperatures from −40°C to 230°C. This is used for ready-meal products to give flexibility in oven or microwave cooking methods
• **Tetra Pak** is a rigid packaging material. It is made from several layers of LDPE (low-density polyethylene – 24%), a layer of aluminium (6%) and paperboard (70%)
• **Gualapack** is a flexible packaging material. It is made from several different plastics: PET, PE, PP (polypropelene), OPA (orientated polyamide) and aluminium.

Both Tetra Paks and Gualapacks are used for liquid food products such as fruit juice, soups and smoothies

[ɪɢ] Coursework

You will need to consider what packaging your final food product will have, but you will not need to design and make it.

❓ Test your knowledge

Describe two types of packaging that use a mixture of materials. What advantages do these mixtures provide?

✏ Activities

1 a Compare the different containers milk is available in such as glass, plastic bottles and Tetra Paks.
b Explain the advantages and disadvantages of each material, including any nutritional benefits.

2 a Compare the packaging used for takeaway foods from a Chinese restaurant and a pizza takeaway.
b Explain the advantages and disadvantages of the types of packaging used.

Summary

★ A variety of materials can be used to package food.

★ The most suitable materials must be chosen to match a particular food product.

Making food products commercially

4.12 Methods of packaging and environmental issues

In this chapter you will:
★ **learn how methods of packaging help to preserve foods**
★ **learn about the environmental impact of packaging.**

Methods of packaging

Aseptic packaging

This method of packaging preserves food without the use of preservatives or refrigeration, making it attractive to **consumers** concerned with 'artificial' foods. It is used to preserve and package all sorts of liquid foods, as well as being an alternative to traditional canning techniques. The food is sterilised outside the package by heating it for 3–15 seconds. The sterile food product is then placed in an air-tight, sterilised package within a hygienic environment. This means that no air is allowed to get to the product once it has been sterilised.

Tetra Pak cartons are often used as the material for this packaging, but plastic bottles can also be used. Most food packaged in this way can be stored for up to six months without refrigeration.

Vacuum packaging

This is a method of packaging that has been used for many years. The air around the food is removed and the plastic package is sealed. The food is kept in anaerobic conditions – this means there is no oxygen around it. This sort of packaging is used for foods such as bacon, fish and coffee.

Modified atmosphere packaging

Modified atmosphere packaging (MAP) is also called controlled atmosphere packaging (CAP). This packaging method extends the **shelf life** by delaying bacterial growth. It involves changing or modifying the usual atmosphere surrounding the food. The air is flushed out and replaced with one or a combination of gases:
• oxygen, which helps to retain the colour of some food, for example meat stays red

• carbon dioxide, which slows the growth of bacteria but is absorbed by foods so can cause the package to collapse
• nitrogen, which is used to replace some of the oxygen so that the rate of oxidation (fruit and vegetables going brown) is reduced.

For products like ready meals, MAP is used in addition to other methods of preservation such as chilling. This means that the shelf life is extended without the use of chemicals – the foods are more 'natural'. Once the package is opened, the food has a normal shelf life.

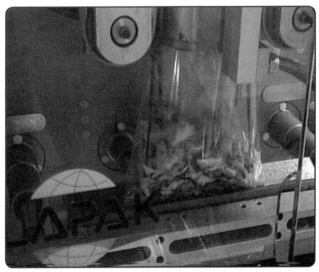
MAP delays bacterial growth

Environmental issues

Sixty per cent of all UK packaging comes from food. This causes a number of environmental problems:
• it uses up natural resources such as oil, trees and metal ore
• it causes air, land and water pollution while it is being made and after it has been used. The process of making can cause chemical gas emissions (gases that damage the environment). The lorries transporting the packaging produce fumes, which also damage the environment
• it cannot always be recycled or it is not all biodegradable, so landfill sites have to be used.

At the moment 90% of rubbish is put into landfill sites. The government wants to reduce this to 30% by 2020. There are also measures in place requiring businesses to take more 'producer responsibility'. There are many ways of reducing the impact of food packaging on the environment:

- Use minimal packaging: manufacturers should use less packaging and consumers should choose products with single-wrapped rather than double-wrapped or triple-wrapped products such as some biscuits.
- Recycle: consumers can use recycling centres or the recycling facilities provided by their local refuse collection service. Manufacturers should use recycled materials such as glass and paperboard. Recycling logos and anti-litter symbols could be printed on the packaging to encourage consumers to recycle.
- Use paperboard: it is biodegradable and comes from a sustainable source. Paperboard can be made from wood grown in managed forests. For every tree cut down for use in production, another is planted.
- Use reusable containers such as jars, egg cartons and plastic bags.

✎ Activities

Think about a product you have recently made.

1 What materials could be used for the packaging? Explain your choices.

2 List the information that would need to be included on the packaging.

Summary

★ Packaging methods can be used as a way of extending the shelf life of foods.

★ Consumers and manufacturers must consider the environmental impact of the food packaging they use.

Case Study

Sainsbury's

Sainsbury's supermarket uses a new packaging material for its organic fruit and vegetables: Potatopak. This type of packaging is already being trialled in several well-known fast-food outlets for burger and other fast-food containers. It is made from potato starch that has been extracted from the water used during the processing of potatoes into crisps, chips and other potato-based products. Therefore, Potatopak is a packaging material made from a waste product. It biodegrades within weeks – even quicker if there is leftover food on the packaging. This material is constantly being developed so that it can withstand high and low temperatures. Perhaps in the near future it will replace plastic as the main packaging material used for food products.

Potatopak is a multi-award winning UK company with manufacturing capabilities in Somerset (UK) and Blenheim (New Zealand). We manufacture innovative 100% biodegradable food serving and packaging products out of potato starch, guaranteed not to last!

Potatopak's driving ambition is to reduce and replace toxic, undesirable, non-biodegradable polystyrene and other plastics from our global ecosystem. The perfect replacement being the 100% safe, 100% biodegradable equivalents made from potato starch waste. Our innovation has achieved much recognition within the growing Green lobby at individual, institutional and governmental levels and we have received a number of awards for our breakthrough products.

Potatopak is committed to helping clean up the environment with a dual approach by utilising the starch from potato processing plants' waste water and converting the waste starch into a product that will help reduce landfill with its biodegradable qualities.

Potatopak packaging is a new development

Introduction to Cauldron Foods

In this chapter you will:
★ learn about Cauldron Foods.

Twenty-two tonnes of soya beans are used every week, ten of which are from organic sources. These are put in quarantine for about a week until the results of a complicated biochemical test for GM, costing £125 a time, has been received.

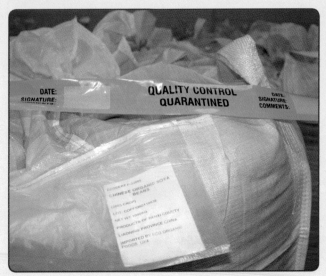

Soya beans in quarantine

History of the company

In 1981 two vegetarians began making their own tofu (soya bean curd) in a garage in Bristol for their own use. Due to growing interest from other vegetarians, a factory was opened to satisfy demand. Supermarkets began to show an interest in the products, so the company moved to their existing premises in Portishead in 1993.

Today, Cauldron employs over 200 people and supplies a range of over 40 vegetarian products to supermarkets and health-food shops. All their products are approved by the Vegetarian Society and use non-GM ingredients. They also produce organic products, which account for 45% of sales, and these are certified by the Soil Association. The total **product range** consists of fourteen sausages, thirteen burgers, six kinds of tofu, fifteen patés and six other products.

Cauldron's ethos

It is estimated that 4–5% of the UK population are true vegetarians. However, 46% of the population are 'meat reducers' – people who decide to eat less meat because of the possible health benefits such as less fat and cholesterol. Cauldron's products are aimed at vegetarians in this broader sense. They aim to produce meat-free products with good **organoleptic properties**. An organic range was introduced in 1999 because **consumer** demand was recognised. This demand is closely tied to vegetarianism, especially with those people who are vegetarians because they are concerned about the damage to the environment. The use of GM foods also has ethical issues, so all ingredients are GM-free.

The company has an environmental policy that aims to reduce the use of energy and harmful emissions during the production process. It also meets the ethical trading and responsible sourcing policies that most major retailers require suppliers to follow. For example, the company makes sure no child labour is used to produce the ingredients. Cauldron also buys their Brazilian soya beans from an area south of the rainforest to avoid deforestation issues.

Marketing Cauldron foods

In recent years the company has expanded and grown from a small to a medium enterprise. Factory space has been increased by 50% and there has been a 10% year-on-year growth in sales, which is unusual for a food manufacturing company. Cauldron now supplies nearly all major supermarkets as well as health-food stores.

A third of Cauldron's **marketing** budget is used to educate consumers about tofu. People usually know what to do with burgers and sausages, but can be unsure about tofu. Leaflets, information booklets and adverts are produced to educate consumers about this product.

SWEET TOFU TEMPTATIONS

Tofu has never been so popular. Health conscious celebrities such as Madonna, Sadie Frost, Moby and Shania Twain incorporate it into their everyday diet. The less starry amongst us are also consuming more tofu, persuaded by its many health benefits and by its versatility as a meal ingredient.

Made from natural soya bean curd, tofu is protein-rich and is cholesterol free, low in saturated fat and contains cholesterol reducing proteins.

Due to its high calcium content, tofu is ideal for people with dairy allergies, vegans, vegetarians and those who just dislike dairy products, and can supply more than four times the calcium of cow's milk.

Tofu also contains isoflavones which are believed to reduce the risk of cancer. Studies have also shown that these isoflavones are a safe and effective natural alternative to HRT for alleviating menopausal symptoms.

Tofu can be flavoured and spiced to make a delicious main meal dish, or puréed to enhance soups or treats such as desserts and cakes. Try this tempting fruity recipe, or for a quick, tasty snack try Cauldron's golden marinated tofu pieces straight from the pack.

Look for Cauldron's ranges of plain, flavoured or smoked GM-free tofu in the chiller cabinets of major supermarkets, independent grocers and health food stores.

cauldron

MOROCCAN DELIGHT

Slimmer's Tip: There are only 99kcal per 100g of Cauldron Plain Tofu

Serves 4

Ingredients
250g pkt Cauldron Organic or Plain
    Tofu, drained and cut into small pieces
1 tbsp finely grated orange rind
1 tbsp clear honey
1-2 tbsp orange juice
12 fresh ripe figs or 4 large ripe peaches
    halved and stoned

Method

1. Place tofu in a food processor with the orange rind and honey. Mix until smooth adding sufficient orange juice to give a creamy consistency.

2. If using figs cut into quarters without cutting right the way through. Gently pull apart. Carefully spoon the creamed tofu into the centre of the fruit. To serve arrange 3 figs or 2 peach halves on each dessert plate.

For a Cauldron tofu recipe leaflet send a stamped addressed AS envelope to: Cauldron Foods Limited, 1-2 Portishead Business Park, Portishead, Bristol BS20 9BF. For further details on tofu visit www.cauldronfoods.co.uk

Adverts and leaflets explain to how to use tofu

Method of production

The factory is in operation 24 hours a day, 7 days a week. Thirty-two hours of each weekend is spent cleaning the factory and equipment.

Tofu, which accounts for 26% of sales and is also used in most other products, is made in the factory in a continuous process. Some of the steps in the process are similar to cheese making. The soya beans are ground twice, water is added and a centrifuge (big spin dryer) is used to separate

Tofu is separated and packaged

the soluble protein (tofu) from the insoluble protein (okara). A chemical coagulant – rather than a biological one as in cheese making – is used to make curds and whey. The curd is pressed and sliced before it is packed.

Other products are batch produced. Large mixers are used for burger, sausage and falafel mixing. Specialist equipment is then used to shape the different products. Some products, such as burgers, falafel and marinated tofu, are deep-fat fried. Sausages are steamed in a temporary casing that is removed once cooled. All products are manually packed into their packaging. Eighty-nine thousand burgers, half a million sausages and seventy thousand packets of tofu are made each week.

Large mixers are used to make the food products

Ic Coursework

You need to show that you understand how food products are manufactured commercially and then relate this to the food products you have designed and made to achieve a good grade.

Activity

Find out about a small-scale or medium-scale food producer near you, or watch a video about a food manufacturer so that it helps with your understanding of food production.

Summary

★ Food production is a complicated business.

★ Some food manufacturers consider the wider implications of their food production such as environmental and ethical issues.

Making food products commercially

In this chapter you will:
★ learn how product development is carried out in a company
★ learn how a manufacturing **specification** is written and used.

All food manufacturers launch new products regularly in order to gain **consumer** interest. These launches are carried out in specific months ready for the autumn, Christmas and spring seasons rather than during the summer months. Cauldron Foods is no exception. The number of products they launch depends on several things such as sales of existing products, suitability of new ideas, demand by retailers and room on their shelves. The product development department works first with **marketing** and later with production to develop ideas.

Initial ideas

New products are initiated in two ways:
- 'blue sky' ideas: these are unusual ideas that are 'plucked' out of the air. There is no theme and no specification. These ideas can be started by group mind mapping. Creativity can also be helped by visiting restaurants, reading food magazines, and buying interesting ingredients – such as unusual vegetables – and experimenting with them in the kitchen. 'Blue sky' ideas mean experimenting with flavour profiles as well as thinking of new products. The ideas are then filtered down and concepts are ready to try in the test kitchen
- new product brief: this is when an idea is identified within the company because of evidence from market research and perceived gaps in the market or from retailers. New product briefs are outline briefs with specific costs of ingredients that must be kept to. Before ideas are tried out, recipes are formulated and costed using spreadsheets. Wastage and yield percentages are included in these budgets. Wastage means how much might be wasted during the production process, so what percentage will be saleable.

Development of ideas

All ideas are tried out and developed again and again in the test kitchen. With the help of **organoleptic** testing, they are continually 'tweaked' until everyone is happy with the new product.

All new ideas are tested in the test kitchen

Good development of ideas comes from experience. Standard recipes are used. If there is a good understanding of the function of ingredients, these can be adapted in different ways. These new product ideas then have to be 'sold' to retailers. They have to be convinced that customers will want to buy them, so they should stock them on their shelves.

An example of a recent product being developed at Cauldron Foods is a mushroom and blue stilton burger, which will be added to the crisp burger range.

A tasting session at Cauldron Foods

Trialling ideas for production

Cauldron Foods uses the actual factory to trial its ideas (some larger factories have a special trial plant). Sixty kilograms of the product is made during each trial. Trialling follows this pattern:

- feasibility trial: a new product feasibility sheet (similar to a product specification sheet) is filled in so that the **nutritional profile** and **shelf life** can be worked out. Organoleptic testing is carried out
- feasibility trial: organoleptic testing is carried out
- feasibility trial: organoleptic testing is carried out again
- pre-production trial: a mini launch to retailers where they taste the product. More organoleptic testing is carried out
- launch of product.

Manufacturing specification

At the pre-production stage, a manufacturing or finished product specification is written.

This specification is very detailed so that the same quality product can be made again and again. The manufacturing specification is part of the **quality control** system. The specification includes:

- product title
- product description
- product weight
- storage conditions
- shelf life
- nutritional composition
- ingredients as a percentage of total
- country of origin
- process information (how the product is made)
- a copy of the **HACCP** data sheet – see page 85
- **critical control points**
- chemical and microbiological standards (the very small amounts of chemicals and bacteria that are allowed to be in the food)
- sensory profile (attributes and description that show appearance, taste and texture required)
- allergen information (for thirteen allergen ingredients)
- suitability for vegetarians, vegans, coeliacs, kosher, halal, organic, GM-free
- packaging information (description, materials including grade, dimensions).

Each ingredient used also has a specification that must be matched when it is delivered to the factory. This specification includes **tolerance levels** that the ingredient must be within such as the amount of moisture nuts or grains can contain or the size of cherry tomatoes used in a burger. This is one way to make sure that the product produced is always the same. This is another quality control.

Therefore, the manufacturing specification contains all the information needed to produce the product in the same way each time it is made.

Coursework

You need to show that you understand how food products are manufactured commercially and then relate this to the food products you have designed and made to achieve a good grade. You also need to be able to write a manufacturing specification for your final product.

? Test your knowledge

In groups, write a manufacturing specification for a product of your choice. Make sure you consider the points outlined on this page.

Summary

★ Product development is a structured process in a food manufacturing company but there are different ways that ideas can be developed.

★ A manufacturing specification is more detailed than a product specification and allows a product to be made in the same way each time it is made.

In this chapter you will:
★ learn to have a better understanding of **HACCP** and **quality controls**.

Using manufacturing **specifications** to ensure quality products are made is just one part of the quality management system (**quality assurance**) that Cauldron Foods follows. Others parts of this system are:
- training workers in hygiene and process procedures
- creating a hygienic working environment
- creating a detailed HACCP.

Training workers

Nearly half of the workforce at Cauldron Foods are from Bristol's Somali community, so instructions are often written in two languages. Visual guides are used for some processes. Detailed hygiene training is given continually, including how to wash hands. In the **high-risk area**, workers must wash their hands twice and use an alcoholic wash after each wash. There are clear instructions for certain processes. For example, when collecting burgers from the deep-fat fryer, the rubber gloves worn must be changed every 30 minutes.

Creating a hygienic environment

There are two main areas of the factory: high risk and low risk. The high-risk area is where the steps in the manufacturing process are carried out after the product has been cooked and before it is sealed into packaging. The warm temperatures are ideal for bacterial growth and there is no further cooking to kill any bacteria. The high-risk area is kept at a temperature below 8°C and the air goes through several filters before it enters the factory to filter out airborne yeasts and bacteria. There are two cleaning shifts at the weekend but the equipment is also cleaned after each batch product is made using high-powered steam and boiling water hoses.

The equipment is cleaned after each batch

Workers make instant biological checks once they have cleaned the equipment to make sure it is bacteria-free. They use a biotrace pen, which they swab the surface of equipment with. This swab is mixed with certain chemicals that react to bacteria by giving out light. This light is measured when the pen is put into a special machine to show the amount of bacteria present. Biotrace pens provide instant results rather than taking swabs and waiting a day or two to see if there is any bacterial growth.

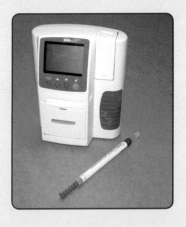

Biotrace pens check for the presence of bacteria

Creating a HACCP

Each food product made has a HACCP document, which is about ten pages long. The three important parts of this document are:
- **hazard** decision tree: the hazards identified at each step of the process are analysed to decide if they are critical. Certain criteria are used to do this such as if there is another process step where this hazard could be checked and how likely the hazard is to happen

- a flow diagram of the process that clearly shows the **critical control points (CCPs)** in red and what they are
- the HACCP data sheet (see example below): this shows the critical control points that have been identified and how they will be controlled.

Critical control points are kept to a minimum and are identified around the factory. For example, the temperature of the tofu is checked after it has been pasteurised. Hand-held temperature probes are used to check temperatures. These probes are connected to a computerised data logging system, which means the temperature is directly input into a computer rather than being written down by the worker.

At Cauldron Foods, five critical control points are identified for the production of tofu:

- CCP1: pasteurised to 86°C for 36 minutes
- CCP2: blast chilled to <10°C within two hours

- CCP3: the seal on the packaging is checked visually (by pressing the package)
- CCP4: the date code is added, showing the 'use by' date
- CCP5: the despatch temperature of the tofu is checked as it goes onto the lorry.

The storage temperature of tofu is important but is not a CCP because the despatch temperature in CCP5 checks the temperature of the product. Refrigeration units, both in the factory and in the lorries, have their own controls and if the temperature goes above a certain level, an alarm is set off.

As the company grows, more hygiene controls may be expected of it. For example, a small sandwich producer is not expected to have a metal detector. But a very large company is now expected to invest in an X-ray machine that would find plastic as well as metal in food products.

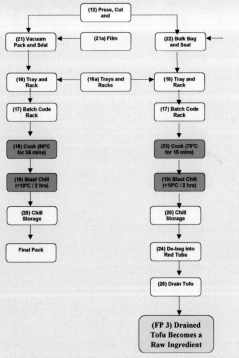

Part of a tofu flow diagram showing some CCP's.

Coursework

You need to show that you understand how food products are manufactured commercially, including how quality controls and HACCP are used. You must then relate this to the food products you have designed and made, and show where quality controls, including HACCP, would be used. This will help you to achieve a good grade.

Activity

Use the system in place at Cauldron Foods to write a detailed HACCP data sheet for a food product you have made.

Summary

★ The use of a quality assurance system, with HACCP at its centre, is vital in the production of quality products for food manufacturers.

CCP number	Process step	Description of CCP	Control measure	Monitoring procedure	Critical limit	Corrective action	Responsibility	Records
1	4	Pasteurisation	Temperature and time controls on oven	Alarm bell for temperature, oven will not open until time has elapsed	86°C for 36 minutes	If temperature and time is not reached, batch is rejected	Production manager	For each batch

Here is one CCP planned out in detail

Making food products commercially

Exam questions

1 Barbecue products use many high-risk foods.
   a Explain what is meant by a high-risk food *(2 marks)*
   b Give three examples of high-risk barbecue foods. *(3 marks)*
   c How does information on a food label help consumers to use and store high-risk foods safely? *(5 marks)*
   (AQA 2003)

2 Explain how to use a food probe to take the temperature of food. *(4 marks)*
   (AQA 2004)

3 **a** Explain why a cake manufacturer uses free-standing electrical equipment for the production of large quantities of cake mixture. *(6 marks)*
   b What health and safety precautions would need to be followed by people using this equipment? *(6 marks)*
   (AQA/NEAB 1999)

4 What is meant by:
   a a critical control point (CCP)? *(2 marks)*
   b a quality control check? *(2 marks)*
   (AQA 2004)

5 The food industry uses standard components to manufacture food products.
   a What do you understand by the term 'standard food components'? *(2 marks)*
   b Explain the advantages and disadvantages of using ready-prepared pizza bases. *(6 marks)*
   (AQA/NEAB 2000)

6 What is meant by batch production? *(3 marks)*
   (AQA 2004)

7 A batch of pastry cases were found to be different sizes and shapes. Explain how control checks could be used during manufacture of the pastry cases to produce consistent results. *(6 marks))*
   (AQA/NEAB 2001)

8 The table opposite shows the main stages of production of a chilled burger product. Complete the chart to show:
   a a different hazard at each stage *(4 marks)*
   b the measures put in place to control each hazard. *(4 marks)*

An example is given.

Stage	Hazard	Control measure
Delivery of raw materials	Biological contamination of food by bacteria	Check date is within 'use by' date
Preparing the burger mixture		
Shaping the burgers		
Chilling the burgers		
Packaging the burgers		

(AQA 2003)

9 Many ready-prepared food products are now packaged for sale.
   a Give four functions of packaging. *(4 marks)*
   b What is Modified Atmosphere Packaging (MAP)? *(2 marks)*
   c Give two different examples of products packaged by this method. *(2 marks)*
   d Discuss the advantages to both the retailer and the consumer of this method of packaging. *(4 marks)*
   e How can manufacturers and consumers show responsibility for the environment when purchasing, using and disposing of packaged food products? *(6 marks)*
   (AQA/NEAB 2000)

10 The cake below has been manufactured for a special occasion. Look at the packaging ideas below.
   a Tick the package you think is the most suitable. Give reasons for your choice. *(4 marks)*
   b On the cake packaging, this is shown: 'This product may contain nuts'. Why is it important to print this information on the label? *(2 marks)*
   c Name three pieces of information that must be printed on a food label. *(3 marks)*
   (AQA/NEAB 2002)

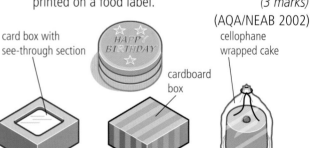

card box with see-through section

cardboard box

cellophane wrapped cake

Idea 1 ☐   Idea 2 ☐   Idea 3 ☐

The structure of food

This section develops the understanding of ingredients learnt in Section 2 by looking at the structure of food.

What's in this section?

In this chapter you will:
★ learn about the structure of sauces.

Using starch to thicken a sauce

Sauces are important food products. They add flavour, colour, moisture and nutritional value to starchy and protein foods. Pasta, rice and potatoes can be boring without a sauce. Meat can also be boring and dry if eaten without a sauce, even if it is just a simple gravy. Therefore, understanding how to create a sauce is important.

Most sauces are thickened by adding starch to liquid. Others can be thickened by the addition of:

- an egg
- an emulsion of oil and water
- a purée of fruit or vegetables.

Some sauces are thickened using a combination of both methods such as a bolognese or ragout. In these cases, tomatoes thicken the sauce but flour makes it nice and rich.

Starchy foods change during cooking:

- with dry heat, such as an oven, starch browns and turns into dextrin (dextrinisation takes place). This reaction is called the Maillard reaction and it happens when bread goes brown when baked or toasted
- with wet heat, such as boiling in liquid, starch goes through the process of gelatinisation. On heating, starch absorbs water and thickens liquids. It makes a sauce.

Gelatinisation

When starch is heated in liquid, the walls of the starch granules become soft and allow the water to pass slowly through them. This makes the granules swell until they get so big with all the water they have absorbed that they burst. This causes the mixture to thicken.

When the starch granules are first mixed in the liquid, they are suspended in the liquid. If the liquid is not stirred, the starch granules stick together and sink to the bottom. When gelatinisation happens, the burst starch granules link together in a network to form a sol. The granules remain dispersed throughout the liquid and do not sink to the bottom. If this sol is allowed to cool, it goes even thicker, setting into a gel as the granules harden.

There are several methods of creating gelatinisation:

- blended sauce: a starch, usually cornflour, is mixed with a liquid and heated. No fat is used, which makes it a bland but low-fat sauce
- all-in-one sauce: a starch, fat and liquid are whisked over heat to make a sauce. This is easy to make but can have a floury aftertaste
- roux sauce: this is the method most chefs use. The fat is melted, then flour is added to make a roux. The mixture is gently cooked for a few minutes before the liquid is gradually added. This method is fairly skilled – it is easy to get a lumpy sauce if the liquid is added too quickly.

Factors affecting the amount of gelatinisation include:

- the type of starch used
- the proportion of starch in relation to liquid
- other ingredients that are added, such as sugar
- the temperature of the liquid
- if the sauce has been stirred while gelatinisation is taking place.

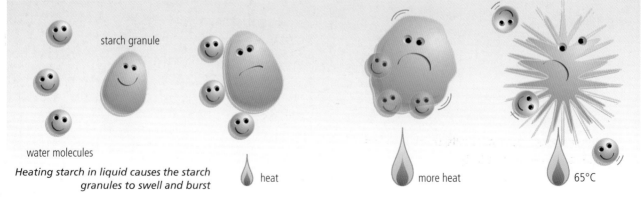

starch granule

water molecules

Heating starch in liquid causes the starch granules to swell and burst

heat

more heat

65°C

Using egg to thicken a sauce

When heated, the protein in egg coagulates. This method is used in real custard (often a little cornflour is used as well) and hollandaise sauce. The sauce must be heated slowly as overcooking causes the mixture to curdle and become lumpy. This method of thickening is also used to make a quiche filling set and to thicken some soups.

Summary

★ Once you understand how to create the structure of a sauce, you can develop one to suit your needs.

Activities

1 Experiment with different starches by making sauces using rice flour, potato flour, cornflour, wheat flour and arrowroot. You could use a 'smart' starch too (see page 35).

   a What differences do these ingredients make to the appearance, texture and taste of the sauces?

   b Chill and freeze the sauces, then defrost and test them again. Do you notice any changes?

2 To gain practical experience of the effects of combining the ingredients looked at in this chapter, make the following dishes:

- macaroni cheese

- bolognese sauce (thickened with flour)

- lasagne.

Analyse and evaluate the results, commenting on appearance, texture and taste.

The structure of food

Gels and foams

In this chapter you will:

★ learn about the structure of gels and foams.

Gels

When a sauce is thickened with starch, a sol is made. When this cools, the sol changes into a gel instead of changing back to its previous state. This means it becomes a solid not a liquid. One example of this is blancmange or powdered custard where cornflour is used.

Sols and gels can also be made from animal proteins such as egg and gelatine. For example, real custard is made from eggs, sugar and milk or cream. When heated, the eggs coagulate to form a gel.

Proteins

Gelatine is a protein extracted from collagen, present in the connective tissue in meat. This means it is unsuitable for vegetarians. It is colourless and almost tasteless. There are two types of gelatine available in the shops:
• powdered gelatine, sold in individual sachets
• leaf gelatine, which is more expensive than powder but leaves less of an aftertaste.

Most jellies are made using gelatine, although vegetarian alternatives are available

Jelly is usually made using protein in the form of gelatine. When heated, the protein melts and is dispersed in the liquid. When this sol starts to cool, the protein molecules unwind and form a network that traps liquid. This forms the gel.

Carbohydrates

Carrageen is a carbohydrate and is extracted from a red seaweed commonly found on the coast of Ireland, making it suitable for vegetarians and vegans.

Agar is another carbohydrate and is the strongest gel-former of all. It comes from an algae that grows off the coast of Japan, so is also suitable for vegetarians and vegans. Jelly can also be made from carrageen or agar instead of gelatine.

Pectin is a gum-like substance that is released from the cell walls of fruit by crushing and cooking at a high temperature, which means it, too, is suitable for vegetarians and vegans. Pectin is used to make jam. It is a complex carbohydrate and is present in most fruit. Once released, this pectin traps sugar, water and fruit to form a gel. Fruit with a high pectin content, such as apples, are often used with other fruits that have a low pectin content such as strawberries and blackberries.

Pectin produces a setting gel that traps the fruit in the jam

Foams

Foams are formed when gas is mixed into a liquid such as whisked egg white and whipped cream. They are aerated mixtures that are made up of small bubbles of gas (usually air) dispersed in a liquid, and they are less stable than gels.

As raw egg white (or liquid cream) is whisked, air bubbles are incorporated into the liquid. The mechanical action of whisking causes proteins to unfold and form a network, which traps the air bubbles and forms a foam. However, these foams are temporary, which means they need something else to happen to them to make them stable.

- If an egg-white foam is heated, the protein in it coagulates and the structure is set. This is a solid foam. Examples of solid foams are meringues, bread (where the gas is carbon dioxide) and cakes (where a mixture of air and carbon dioxide are used).
- If the foam is not going to be cooked, something extra needs to be added to make the product into a solid foam. Gelatine is often used in mousses and cheesecakes to set the mixture.

Meringues are a common example of foams, and are used in desserts such as a pavlova. There are three different methods of making meringues:

1 *Swiss meringue* (the one most frequently made as it is the easiest) is when the egg white is whisked until stiff. Then the sugar is folded in.

Pavlovas are solid foams where the egg white has been heated to form a solid structure

2 *Cuite meringue* is when icing sugar is sieved onto the egg whites in a bowl. This bowl is then placed over a pan of simmering water and whisked until the mixture is thick and holds its shape. This meringue is firmer than Swiss meringue and is used for meringue baskets.

3 *Italian meringue* is when syrup made out of sugar and water is poured onto whisked egg white and whisked in thoroughly. It is used as a topping or filling for cakes or to replace cream. It is difficult to make and requires the use of a sugar thermometer as the syrup has to be 260° F.

Activities

1 Make two set fruit blancmanges using milk as the liquid and fresh or tinned strawberries to add flavour. Make one using cornflour to set the mixture into a gel and the other using gelatine. Leave both to chill in the fridge and compare them in your next lesson, commenting on appearance, texture and taste.

2 Experiment with the quantities of cornflour and vinegar that can be added to meringue to produce a perfect Pavlova base. How did the ingredients affect the result?

3 To gain practical experience of the effects of combining the ingredients looked at in this chapter, make a fruit mousse using a protein and whipped cream. Use nutritional analysis to look at the nutritional make-up of the mousse.

Summary

★ Foams and gels are interesting ways to form structure in a food product.

The structure of food

Coagulation of proteins

In this chapter you will:

★ learn about the coagulation of protein foods.

Protein foods are important foods in our diet. You need to understand the function and structure of these foods. The main protein foods are meat, poultry, fish, eggs, and dairy products.

Eggs

Eggs have lots of uses and functions in cooking:
- aeration: whisking egg traps air in mixtures such as cakes
- foam: egg whites make a foam by trapping air when whisked
- emulsification: they allow oil and water to mix together
- glazing on pastry: the egg turns the pastry golden brown during cooking
- binding: egg coagulates when heated –this means it sticks ingredients, such as biscuits and cakes, together as they cook
- thickening: the addition of egg thickens sauces
- coating: egg sticks breadcrumbs together to seal food, such as fish, when it is deep fried.

Meat, poultry and fish

These are the muscle tissue of animal (meat), birds (poultry) and fish. The internal organs, such as liver, kidney and heart, are known as offal. This tissue contains protein, water, vitamins and minerals. The protein in the muscle tissue coagulates during cooking to set.

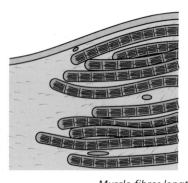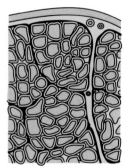

Muscle fibres lengthways and in cross-section

The muscle tissue of meat and poultry is made up of long, thin muscle fibres. These fibres are held together in bundles by connective tissue. There are two types of connective tissue:
- collagen, which holds the bundles of muscle fibres together. When it is heated, it dissolves to gelatine
- elastin, which binds the muscle together or to a bone. It is tougher than collagen, does not dissolve when heated and is slightly yellow in colour. It provides elasticity and strength.

The muscle flesh of fish is made up of bundles of short muscle fibres held together by collagen. There is no elastin in fish.

Tenderness

The length and size of muscle fibres determine how tender or tough meat will be. This should have a bearing on how the meat should be cooked. The amount of fat in the muscle also has some effect on tenderness, as this melts during cooking to expose more collagen, which dissolves to gelatine.

The muscle tissue from different parts of animals and birds has different lengths of muscle fibres and different amounts of connective tissue. The muscle with the longest fibres and the most connective tissue comes from the parts of the body that do the most work such as the legs or shoulders. This can be the toughest meat, so it needs longer to cook. It is usually better to cook this meat slowly in a liquid rather than by dry heat.

Fish needs a short cooking time because of the short muscle fibres and small amount of connective tissue.

Cooking makes meat tender but there are other ways to help tenderise it:
- cutting or mincing meat with long muscles to make mince, stewing or braising steak
- beating with a meat hammer to separate the fibres or scoring across the fibres with a knife
- marinating in acid-based liquids, such as lemon juice and vinegar, to soften the collagen.

Other characteristics of meat

Myoglobin is the colour pigment that causes the colour of raw meat to be red or purplish. It is found more in muscle tissues that are used the most such as legs, thighs and shoulders. When the meat is cooked to above 65°C, the colour changes to brown.

As the protein coagulates, moisture is squeezed out and meat juices appear. These add flavour to cooking liquids and gravy, or evaporate on grilled or roasted meat to leave an aromatic coating.

Overcooking by dry heat methods can make the muscle fibres hard and tough. This is true for fish as well as for meat and poultry.

The nutritional value of meat, poultry and fish should also be considered. All these contain high biological value proteins.

Red meat is high in iron and calcium. White fish and white poultry meat are low in fat. Oily fish contain good amounts of essential fatty acids Omega 3.

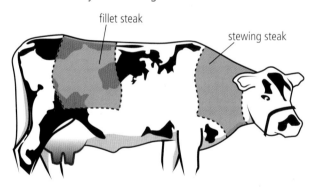

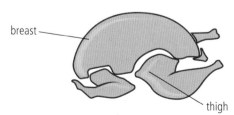

Turkey and beef: the least tender and the leanest joints

Activities

1 Use different meats to make burgers so that you have practical experience of the different appearance and flavours these meats provide. Experiment with mixing meats; for example, make a pork and beef burger. How did each burger turn out? Write notes, commenting on appearance, texture and taste.

2 To gain practical experience of the working characteristics of food discussed in this chapter, make:
   - a curry using cheap, tough cuts of meat that need slow, long cooking

   - a number of kebabs using a variety of marinades to show how these tenderise meat.

   - fishcakes using a variety of fish such as tuna, salmon, cod, and coley.

   Assess the outcome of these dishes. How did your curry taste? Which marinade worked best?

Summary

★ Meat makes up an important part of most main course food products for non-vegetarians. It is important to understand how its structure can be manipulated.

The structure of food

Alternative proteins

Most of the protein in a non-vegetarian **diet** comes from animals: either their meat (from fish, poultry, and so on) or from eggs and dairy products. If you eat these foods, you get enough protein in your diet.

Most vegetarians get their protein by eating eggs and dairy products, even if this lacks variety. Vegans need to eat other sources of protein. These sources of alternative proteins can be divided into two groups:

- *alternative protein foods*: foods used instead of meat to provide the necessary protein in the diet
- *meat analogues or replacements*: foods that provide protein and can be used in the same way as meat but are made from vegetable sources.

Of course, all of these proteins can also be eaten by meat eaters.

Alternative proteins

All vegetables contain some protein but pulses (beans and lentils) and nuts contain the most. Grains are quite a good source too.

Nuts and pulses (beans and lentils) are the vegetables with the highest amount of protein in them. These vegetable proteins are low biological value (LBV) proteins. All except one of the vegetable proteins (soya bean) have at least one or more essential amino acids missing, which means that if eaten on their own, the body cannot use this protein. If the body is to use this vegetable protein, a mixture of vegetables must be eaten together to complement each other. For example, a variety of beans could be used in a chilli sin carne (chilli without meat) and then served with rice, or a nut burger could be made containing nuts, peas and sweetcorn so there is a mixture of proteins as well as tastes.

Lentils	Beans	Others
puy	cannellini	chickpeas
green	harricot	peas
brown	brown	gunga or pigeon
red split	black eye	peas
Dal (Indian	flageolet	black peas
name for lentil)	butter	
channa	mung	
urid	aduki	
	borlotti	
	pinto	
	red kidney	
	moth	
	rosecoco	

Here are just some of the pulses grown around the world

Meat analogues

Many new vegetarian products are based on meat replacements. These are products that are manufactured in such a way that they look and taste like meat.

Quorn is a myco-protein. It is a tiny fungus that is grown in a glucose mix in a large fermenting vat. Extra vitamins are added and vegetable flavours mixed in. It is then rolled into sheets and set by steaming. The product is then processed into shapes: it is cubed, sliced, shredded or minced.

Quorn has the following characteristics.

- The texture is similar to chicken. It can be processed to taste like chicken or ham.
- It lacks its own flavour but it absorbs surrounding flavours well.
- It is high in protein and low in fat.

Meat analogues can be used in the same way as meat but are made from vegetable sources

- It contains more fibre than meat but this is still a small amount.
- It is unsuitable for vegans as egg white is used in the manufacturing process.

TVP (textured vegetable protein) is made from soya beans. It is the only vegetable protein to have a high biological value (HBV), which means no essential amino acids are missing, so the body can use the protein. TVP is made from the soya bean once the oil has been taken out. The remaining bean is ground into flour. This flour is mixed into dough with water and forced through a small hole (extruded) under pressure at a high temperature. This dough can be extruded through shaped nozzles to produce chunks, flakes and grains.

TVP has the following characteristics.
- It has a bland flavour. Flavourings can be added or it can be cooked with distinctive flavoured foods such as tomatoes, curry spices, garlic and herbs.
- It can be dried, frozen or chilled.
- It is high in protein and dietary fibre.
- It is low in fat.
- It is fortified with vitamin B and iron.

TVP is used as a meat alternative but it is also often used as a bulking ingredient. This is because it is less expensive than animal proteins such as meat. So, if TVP is used

instead of meat a 'value' product can be made. 'Economy' burgers are an example of a food product that uses TVP for this purpose.

Tofu is another alternative protein food product made from the soya bean, but it does not have the appearance or texture of meat. It is made by curdling soya milk with calcium sulphate, separating it into a solid and a liquid. The solid produced in this process is called tofu. It is a soft, smooth textured, semi-solid food that has very little flavour of its own. It is high in protein and low in fat. Tofu can also be marinated to give it more flavour. It can also be used in silken form (runny) where it could be used as an alternative to cream or cheese in desserts.

Other branded meat replacements

There are several other branded food products available that use a mixture of ingredients to provide the protein and texture needed. Realeat vegetarian mince is a mixture of wheat and soya protein. Linda McCartney's vegetarian sausages contain pea and wheat protein.

Activities

1 Experiment with different meat analogues available. Make a spaghetti bolognese using at least three different analogues. Use sensory analysis techniques to evaluate the results.

2 Carry out your own research into what meat replacement products are widely available from supermarkets.

Test your knowledge

1 Which vegetables have the highest amount of protein in them?

2 Describe what TVP is and how it is made.

Summary

★ Alternative proteins have to be considered when food manufacturers design vegetarian products.

The structure of food

Emulsions

In this chapter you will:
★ **learn about the general structure of foods, including colloidal structures**
★ **learn about one of these structures – emulsions.**

Food structures can be divided into two groups:
- primary foods such as meat, fish, eggs, vegetables and fruit. This is where the basic cell structure of the food is unchanged when eaten
- processed foods such as butter made from milk, jam made from fruit and sugar, and sausages made from meat, spices and rusk.

Colloids

We eat many processed foods. They are made from primary foods. Bread is made from wheat and cheese from milk. Nearly all processed foods are made from more than one ingredient and nearly all of them have a colloidal structure. Colloids are formed when two substances are mixed together, such as flour and water, but the substances do not combine to form a solution, which happens, for example, with salt in water. A colloid is formed because the molecules are too big to form a solution. This colloidal mixture gives structure, texture and mouth feel to many products. The main types of colloidal structures are given in the table below.

Colloidal structure	What it consists of	Examples
Sol	Solid dispersed in liquid	Unset jelly, hot cheese sauce, warm custard
Gel	Liquid dispersed in solid	Set jelly, cold custard, jam, blancmange
Foam	Gas dispersed in liquid	Whipped cream, whisked egg white
Solid foam	Gas dispersed in solid	Meringue, bread, cake, ice cream
Liquid emulsion	Liquid dispersed in liquid	Mayonnaise, milk
Solid emulsion	Liquid dispersed in solid	Butter, margarine

The main types of colloidal structure

Emulsions

Emulsions are one kind of colloidal structure. Liquids such as oil and water do not mix. If left to stand, they form two separate layers as the oil rises above the water. As you can see in the table, there are two types of emulsion:
- liquid emulsions, such as oil and vinegar
- solid emulsions, such as fat-free milk beaten into a blend of oil to make margarine.

There are two types of liquid emulsion:
- unstable emulsion, such as vinaigrette or French dressing, where the liquids quickly separate
- stable emulsion, such as mayonnaise, where the ingredients combine.

Unstable emulsions

Salad dressings are good examples of unstable emulsions. They add flavour, mouth feel and texture to salads. It is important to add the right dressing to each salad.

Salad dressings

The foundation of a good dressing is the oil. This can be one or a mixture of oils. Olive oil is popular, but nut oils, such as walnut, give good flavour.

Vinegar is also used in salad dressings. This can be red or white wine, cider, balsamic or a fruit vinegar. Again, more than one type can be used to make a dressing. Lemon juice can also be used as well as or instead of vinegar.

Extra ingredients are added. These are usually mustard and salt and pepper. All sorts of other ingredients can also be added to develop a standard recipe such as herbs, garlic, spices, cheese, tomatoes, yoghurt and cream.

Stable emulsions

A stable emulsion has an extra substance added to stop the oil and water from separating. This extra ingredient is called an emulsifier. Emulsifier molecules have a water-loving (hydrophilic) head and a water-hating (hydrophobic) tail. These molecules lower the surface tension between the two liquids so that they combine to form a stable emulsion.

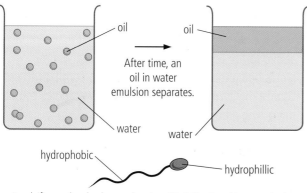

After time, an oil in water emulsion separates.

Emulsifier molecules have a head and tail. The head is water-loving (hydrophillic) where as the tail is water-hating (hydrophobic).

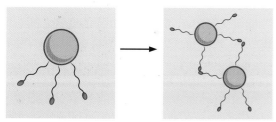

The head is attracted to the water because it is water-loving. The water-hating tail is attracted to the oil droplets.

This means the emulsifier molecules gather round the oil droplets and stop them from separating out from water.

Emulsifier molecules help to form stable emulsions

Emulsifiers

There are many artificial emulsifiers used by the food industry. Glycerol monostearate (GMS) is one example that is used in large-scale manufacture. Lecithin in egg yolk is a natural emulsifier used to make mayonnaise a stable emulsion. Lecithin is also found in soya beans.

Eggs are used as a natural emulsifier, not only in mayonnaise but also in cakes and biscuits. In the creaming method, the egg is added to a mixture of fat and sugar. If the egg is added cold or all at once, the emulsion will not form and the mixture looks as if it has curdled. The fat becomes solid and appears as if it is floating in the egg.

Activities

1 Research different salad dressing recipes. Make two or three of the most interesting you have found.

2 To gain practical experience of the effects of combining the ingredients looked at in this chapter, make the following dishes:

- Caesar salad
- coleslaw with real mayonnaise.

How did each dressing turn out? Write notes, commenting on appearance, texture and taste.

Summary

★ It is important that you understand how colloidal structures can be used when making food products.

Smart and modern ingredients

> In this chapter you will:
> ★ learn more about smart and modern materials that food manufacturers use to create the required structure of a product.

Smart ingredients have been looked at on page 35, where information about materials that can be used in baking products was given. Here we will look at a different range of smart ingredients.

Smart ingredients

Smart ingredients are not natural ingredients; they have been developed through the invention of new and improved processes. The word 'smart' is not used in food manufacturing, but it is a good general term to use to identify and group together these kinds of ingredients.

Why are smart ingredients used?

Despite the wide range of food ingredients available, food manufacturers often want to make a food product with a structure, taste, appearance or texture that cannot be achieved using existing ingredients. Therefore, they use new and modern technology to create ingredients that will behave in the way they want them to. Some of these ingredients have been available for many years.

Some meat analogues are smart ingredients because they are manufactured in such a way that the taste, appearance and mouth feel is just like meat. One example is Quorn, which is made to look and taste like chicken.

Modified starches

The biggest range of smart ingredients available today are smart (modified) starches. There are over 300 modified starches available for use in a wide range of food products.

These starches may be modified by physical means such as heating and shearing (beating vigorously), or by chemical treatment such as oxidation and hydrolysis (where oxygen and hydrogen are added to the starch molecules).

Consumer starches

Sauce flour and thickening granules

Very few smart starches are available to **consumers** as individual ingredients on their own and not incorporated into food products. Two examples are:

- sauce flour, which is wheat flour that does not form lumps when making a sauce – it has been modified physically to do this. New technology in the milling process has allowed this to happen
- thickening granules, which is maize starch that can be added to hot liquids to make them thicken without lumps being formed. If you add ordinary cornflour to hot liquids, the liquid becomes lumpy. Gravy granules contain thickening granules and flavourings.

Manufactured starches

All of the 300 or so modified starches are used by manufacturers during the food manufacturing process. They can be divided into pre-gelatinised starches and chemically modified starches.

Pre-gelatinised starches are modified in the sense that they are processed to behave differently from ordinary cornflour or wheat flour. They are pre-cooked starches. They are heated up in liquid until they become thick. They are then cooled and spray-dried into tiny granules. Around 50 of these starches are available. They have an off-white, grainy texture compared to ordinary flours and sometimes have a slight aftertaste. They are used in instant foods that people can add liquid to and eat straightaway such as instant whip, instant custard, Cup-a-Soups and Pot Noodles.

An example of a non-food use for this kind of starch is wallpaper paste. Cold liquid is added to a powder and it instantly becomes a sticky paste.

Chemically modified starches make up the biggest range of smart starches. These are modified to behave in all sorts of ways, so that they:
- stay runny when the product is chilled, such as a chilled lasagne
- prevent syneresis (water leaking out of the sauce) during freezing, such as frozen macaroni cheese
- thicken without heating
- remain unaffected by acid or sugar – they do not go runny when these are added, such as fruit pie fillings
- remain stable during processing – for example, they do not go runny when beaten rigorously
- have mouth feel properties similar to fat so that a small amount could be used instead of fat in a sauce – for a low-fat product

---

INGREDIENTS: Sugar, Hydrogenated Vegetable Oil, Modified Starch, Emulsifiers (Propane-1, 2-diol esters of fatty acids, Soya Lecithin), Gelling Agents (Disodium Phosphate, Diphosphates), Milk Protein, Lactose, Flavourings, Colours (Betanin, Annatto, Beta-Carotene), Whey Powder.
NO ARTIFICIAL COLOURS OR PRESERVATIVES

Added Ingredients
Strawberry: Strawberry (8%), Oligofructose, Modified Starch, Acidity Regulators: Citric Acid, Sc Sweeteners: Aspartame, Acesulfame K.

Raspberry: Raspberry (6%), Oligofructose, Modified Starch, Acidity Regulators: Sodium Citrate, Sweeteners: Aspartame, Acesulfame K.

Black Cherry: Black Cherry (10%), Oligofructose, Modified Starch, Flavouring, Acidity Regulator Artificial Sweeteners: Aspartame, Acesulfame K.

Peach: Peach (8%), Oligofructose, Modified Starch, Flavouring, Thickener: Fruit Pectin; Acidity Re Sweeteners: Aspartame, Acesulfame K.

INGREDIENTS
BEANS (49%), TOMATOES (27%), WATER, SUGAR, MODIFIED MAIZE STARCH, SALT, ONION POWDER, PAPRIKA, HERB EXTRACTS, SPICE EXTRACTS.

Modified starches are used by food manufacturers in many products

---

- provide a source of NSP (fibre) without the disadvantages of using wholemeal flours, such as high fibre flour.

Two examples of these starches only available to food manufacturers are:
- Firm-tex. This can be used in hotdog manufacturing as it reduces shrinkage and drip and also has excellent freeze/thaw stability.
- N-Tack. This can be used as a coating for dry roasted nuts. This is quick drying and has a high degree of tackiness so it provides a thin, uniform coating.

Activities

1. Use a range of different 'flours', including sauce flour and thickening granules, to make a basic white sauce. Analyse and evaluate the results.

2. Use sensory analysis to compare products, such as soup or custard, made using conventional starch and those made using pre-gelatinised starch.

3. To gain practical experience of the working characteristics of food and the effects of combining the ingredients looked at in this chapter, use preglatinised starch to make a few instant desserts using different fruits and other flavourings. Use sensory analysis to evaluate them and compare them with products that do not use pre-gelatinised starch.

Summary

★ Manufacturers use smart and modern materials to increase the range of food products available.

Cooking choices

> **In this chapter you will:**
> ★ learn how cooking can affect the structure of food.

The characteristics and structure of certain foods can be altered by the transfer of heat to foods. Food is cooked to:
- make it more digestible: heat softens the cell structure of vegetables and fruit, for example potatoes
- improve the flavour, for example roast potatoes
- improve the texture, for example toast
- improve the smell, for example bread, coffee beans.

There are many different ways that food can be cooked.

Cooking with liquid

This is cooking with water or other liquids such as milk or stock.
- Boiling: foods, such as vegetables, are boiled vigorously in water in a saucepan. This kind of cooking uses convection heating, where heat is exchanged through a liquid or gas such as boiling potatoes in hot water.
- Simmering: foods that need more gentle cooking, such as eggs, curries and stews, are cooked slowly in liquids.
- Steaming: foods are cooked in steamers over boiling water. This is a popular method for vegetables because water-soluble vitamins do not leak out into the water.
- Sweating: a form of steaming where no liquid is used except for the steam coming off the food – onions are sometimes cooked in this way. The pan lid must be on to make this method work.

Steaming is just one cooking method

Frying

Different fats are used to fry food to add flavour during the cooking process. Fat heats to a higher temperature than water or other liquids, so the food cooks quickly and often becomes crispy. Some of the fat is absorbed by the food, so the energy content and fat content of the food increases. For example, chips have a higher energy value than boiled potatoes.

- Deep-fat frying: the whole food is immersed in hot fat. This method is used in fish and chip shops. However, delicate foods such as fish need to be protected with batter or breadcrumbs.
- Shallow frying: just a little oil is used for foods such as eggs or mushrooms.
- Dry frying: becoming popular because no oil is added. The fat within the food, for example in bacon and burgers, is used for frying. Often a griddle is used so that the fat runs away from the food.
- Wok frying: similar to dry frying. A very small amount of oil (or stock) might be used to lubricate the pan. Cooking is by conduction – heat is in direct contact with the food. Stir-fry dishes are cooked in this way. The food must be moved continuously to stop it sticking or burning.

Wok frying is similar to dry frying

Oven cooking

- Baking: foods are cooked on their own in an oven. Cakes, bread, biscuits, baked potatoes and whole fish are examples of cooking this way.
- Roasting: this is when foods are basted with fat during cooking. This basting improves the flavour of the food. Meat, poultry and potatoes are often cooked this way.

Direct-heat cooking

- Grilling: a quick method of cooking where heat is directed straight onto the food. Sausages, fish and toast can be cooked this way. This method of cooking uses radiation to transfer heat. Infrared heat rays pass through the air until they come into contact with the food.
- Microwave cooking: also uses direct heat but the rays used are different to grilling. They are electromagnetic radiation of high energy and short wavelengths. They quickly heat anything containing liquid by causing the liquid to vibrate, producing heat.

Choosing equipment

It is important to choose suitable equipment to prepare food ingredients. You could prepare ingredients by hand or use small-scale equipment for some processes. Think about what equipment is the best to use to produce quality products. The table below summarises these methods.

? Test your knowledge

Draw up a table to summarise the advantages and disadvantages of the different methods of frying.

✎ Activity

To gain practical experience of the working characteristics of food looked at in this chapter, make two chocolate cakes, cooking one in a microwave and one in an oven. Analyse and evaluate the results, commenting on appearance, texture, taste and convenience.

Summary

★ There are many different methods of cooking that can be used to create different structures in food. You need to think about these cooking methods when designing food products.

Process	Hand method	Machinery method
Peeling, cutting, chopping	Use different knives or peelers	The chopping blade in the food processor chops food finely, and the slicing blade slices food such as cucumber
Mixing	Mix doughs and pastry in a mixing bowl	Use the food processor or a large electric food mixer to mix the dough in one step
Shaping	Use tools to cut melon balls, shape meatballs and cut biscuit shapes	Use the food processor attachment to make sausages
Grating	Use a hand grater or Mouli grater to grate cheese, carrots, potatoes	Use the grating attachment on the food processor to grate, or a special electric food grater
Whisking	Use a rotary whisk or balloon whisk to beat egg white and cream	Use an electric whisk to beat ingredients quickly
Making pasta	Roll and cut the pasta	Use a pasta-making machine to extrude the dough into strips

The structure of food

Preservation 1: High temperature and chemical methods

> **In this chapter you will:**
> ★ learn about preservation and why it is important
> ★ consider how some methods of preservation work.

Cooking changes the characteristics of food – their structure, taste, texture and appearance. Heat also destroys bacteria and enzymes, which trigger chemical reactions. This means cooking extends the **shelf life** of food, helping it last longer.

However, some raw foods need to be preserved because they do not stay fresh and safe to eat for long. Preservation helps to extend the shelf life of these foods.

High temperature methods of preservation

Using heat is one method of preservation. There are several ways heat is used to preserve food.

Canning

This is a traditional method of preservation, destroying bacteria by heating. It involves sterilising food in airtight containers to prevent recontamination. In commercial food manufacture, the cans are filled automatically before liquid is added. The cans are then sealed under a vacuum so that the air at the top of the can is drawn out. Batches of cans are heated to 121°C in a large pressure cooker. The cans are cooled using cold water sprays and cooling tanks so that the food does not overcook. As canning involves heating foods to high temperatures it changes the characteristics of these foods.

A good example of the effect canning has on food is peaches. The texture and flavour of tinned peaches is quite different to fresh peaches.

Bottling

Bottling is similar to canning and is often carried out at home. Fruit and vegetables are put in glass bottles. Water is added and the jars are heated in an oven. The lid is put on to give them an airtight seal.

The art of bottling fruit and vegetables in the summer (while there is so much around) is dying out in the UK. In France, households still bottle fruit and vegetables such as green beans. Supermarkets have whole shelves of bottling jars and other equipment.

Pasteurisation, sterilisation and ultra heat treatment (UHT)

These methods of heating are used with liquids, particularly milk and fruit juice:

- pasteurisation: the milk is heated to 72°C for 15 seconds, then rapidly cooled to 10°C. This method kills pathogenic (food-poisoning) bacteria so is not a long-term method of preservation
- sterilisation: the liquid is heated to 104°C for 40 minutes or 113°C for 15 minutes. This kills nearly all micro-organisms and enzymes. It also changes the flavour and colour of the milk or juice
- UHT: the liquid, usually milk, is heated to 130–150°C for 1–3 seconds. The process means that nearly all micro-organisms and enzymes are killed, but there is little change in the flavour and colour of the food.

Milk is available in many forms

Irradiation

This is a new method of preservation, introduced into the UK in the 1990s. Food is hit with ionising radiation (similar to X-rays), which kills or reduces micro-organisms, delays the ripening of fruit and the sprouting of vegetables. At present, only herbs and spices are irradiated. By law, all irradiated food must be labelled as such.

Chemical methods of preservation

Bacteria need water to grow and many also need a neutral pH (6.6–7.5). Therefore, if the liquid around food is not neutral, bacteria will not grow. Below is a list of ways that different chemicals are used to change the pH and therefore preserve food.

- Salting is used to preserve fish and meat. Salt absorbs the water from the food so there is none left for the bacteria.
- Sugar is used for jams and jellies. Bacteria do not thrive in high levels of sugar.
- Vinegar is acidic so bacteria do not thrive. Pickles, chutneys or whole and sliced vegetables such as onions and beetroot are pickled in vinegar. Lemon juice is also acidic and is used as a short-term method of preserving fruit salads.
- Spices are used to preserve cooked meats, such as salami, as they prevent bacterial growth.
- Fermentation that produces alcohol or acids is a form of preservation. This helps with the preservation of some cheeses and yoghurt. It also means that soy sauce (fermented from soya beans), beer and wine last a long time.
- Alcohol does not have a neutral pH, so it is used to preserve fruits such as peaches in brandy.
- Smoking is a way of preserving fish and meat. The effects of the smoke and the heat help to destroy bacteria.
- Preservatives such as sodium nitrite, used to make bacon out of pork, are chemicals that stop the growth of bacteria.

Some chemical methods of preservation

Activities

1   Complete a sensory analysis on a selection of the preserved milks available.

2   To gain practical experience of how to preserve foods looked at in this chapter, make lemon curd or jam using a microwave to speed up the cooking. Analyse and evaluate the results, commenting on appearance, texture and taste.

Summary

★ Preservation methods affect the quality and storage of food.

★ The use of high temperatures and chemicals are two methods of preservation.

★ Methods of storage and preservation need to be considered when designing food products.

5.9 Preservation 2: Low temperature and drying methods

> **In this chapter you will:**
> ★ continue to learn about different preservation methods.

There are other methods of preservation as well as heat.

Drying

Drying is probably the oldest method of preservation. Nearly all the water is removed from the food – as micro-organisms need liquid to grow, the removal of water preserves the food. Many fruits, such as apricots and figs, are dried. Different grapes are dried to make sultanas, raisins and currants. Some vegetables are dried such as tomatoes, chillies and peppers. These kinds of foods are often sun-dried, which means they are left to dry naturally in the sun.

Commercial drying of food is usually done by the most modern method: accelerated freeze drying (AFD). This is where food is dried inside a vacuum at reduced pressure. The food is frozen and then heated quickly. The ice changes to steam without passing through the liquid stage. This process preserves most of the flavour, colour and texture of the food, and the food does not shrink as much as in other methods of drying.

All sorts of foods are dried: fruit added to breakfast cereals, vegetables, meat and fish in ready meals, Pot Noodles and Cup-a-Soups, coffee, herbs and dog food.

Dried foods are good because:
- they can be stored long term
- they can be eaten out of season

Many food products are dried to preserve them

- they weigh less than standard foods and occupy less space (useful for people travelling)
- some dried foods, such as prunes and sultanas, taste different from fresh fruit
- they retain most of their nutrients
- dried pulses, such as beans and lentils, are valuable sources of protein and high in NSP (dietary fibre).

Freezing

Today we have fridges and freezers that help to preserve food. Cold temperatures are used to slow down or stop bacterial growth. If you look back to page 65, you will see that bacteria like warmth to grow fast.

Freezing was first used in China in 1800 BC. Freezing turns liquids, such as water, into solids, such as ice. As micro-organisms need liquid as a well as warmth to grow, this makes freezing a long-term method of preservation. Factories where food is frozen use three basic methods:
- plate freezing: flat products, such as burgers and fish fingers, are frozen between two plates
- blast freezing: freezing air is blasted over irregular shaped foods such as vegetables and prawns
- cryogenic or immersion freezing: food is immersed or sprayed with liquid nitrogen. This is an expensive method and is usually used only for delicate foods such as raspberries.

Chilling

Chilling is a temporary or short-term method of preservation. Chilled food is usually kept just above 0 °C. Because the temperature is low, the rate of bacterial

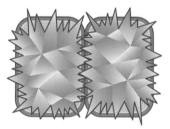

slow freezing produces large ice crystals which break the cell walls in the food.

Quick freezing produces smaller ice crystals so there is less damage to cell walls.

Modern methods of freezing allow small ice crystals to form

Method of preservation	Advantages	Disadvantages
Freezing	• Long-term method of preservation (weeks and months rather than days) • Little change in flavour or structure compared to canned or dried food • Very little nutritional loss – most vitamin B and C is retained	• Quick and controlled freezing is needed or large ice crystals will form and break the cell walls of some foods • Vegetables need to be blanched (immersed quickly in boiling water) or enzymes will continue to work and change the flavour and texture of the food • Specialist storage equipment is needed – a freezer kept at below −18°C. Long-term stores must be below −26°C • Flavours of garlic, spices and herbs often become stronger during freezing. This needs to be taken into account when designing food • Cell damage can occur in soft fruits such as strawberries, and the colloidal structure of some food products, such as sauces, can collapse when frozen
Chilling	• Taste closer to fresh foods than frozen, canned or dried foods • There is little loss of flavour, colour, texture, shape or nutritional value • Allows **consumers** to have good quality, ready-prepared food without having to shop every day	• Only a temporary, short-term method of preservation • Specialist storage equipment is needed – a fridge kept at below 5°C. Commercial stores must be below 2°C

The advantages and disadvantages to freezing and chilling

growth is reduced but not stopped. Chilled foods can be a single food or a food product such as a ready meal. These **cook-chill foods** are prepared, cooked and chilled rapidly. Once cooked, they must be blast-chilled to a temperature below 5°C within 90 minutes. They must then be stored at this temperature until they are reheated for use. Cook-chill foods can be stored only for a few days, although if special packaging is used, their **shelf life** can be extended to up to 14 days. The food should be reheated until the centre reaches at least 72°C and eaten within two hours.

The different types of preservation have different advantages and disadvantages and are suitable for different foods. The table above summarises the advantages and disadvantages of freezing and chilling as methods of preservation.

Activity

To gain practical experience of how to use preserved foods looked at in this chapter, design and make a dried soup using a variety of dried vegetables, herbs and spices, powdered stock and pre-gelatinised starch. Analyse and evaluate the results, commenting on appearance, texture and taste.

Summary

★ Preservation methods affect the quality and storage of food.

★ Drying and the use of low temperatures are two methods of preservation.

★ Methods of storage and preservation need to be considered when designing food products.

Test your knowledge

1 Explain why a consumer might prefer chilled to frozen food.

2 In which situations would using dried foods be an advantage?

3 What are the advantages of using canned rather than frozen foods?

Exam questions

1 During the development and testing of products, the following comments were made. Give one way of improving each product and a reason for your improvement.

  a Comment: *The beef burger crumbles when cooking.*
    Improvement.   *(2 marks)*
    Reason.   *(2 marks)*

  b Comment: *The spring rolls are uneven in size and shape.*
    Improvement.   *(2 marks)*
    Reason.   *(2 marks)*
                               (AQA/NEAB 2000)

2 When a flour-based sauce mixture is heated, the starch thickens the milk by a process of gelatinisation.

  a Explain the process of gelatinisation.

  b What will happen if gelatinisation does not take place?   *(5 marks)*
                                (AQA/NEAB 2000)

3 Eggs are an important ingredient in the manufacture of many products. Complete the chart below to explain the use of eggs in the preparation and cooking of the named product. An example is given for you.   *(8 marks)*

Product	Use of an egg in preparation and cooking
Mousse – cream with egg white and gelatine	Eggs trap air when whisked, making products light and fluffy in texture
Meringue – whisked egg white with sugar	
Cheese flan with egg and milk filling	
Fish cakes coated in egg and breadcrumbs	
Mayonnaise – an egg and oil sauce	

                                (AQA/NEAB 2002)

Food choices and needs

This section develops the knowledge and understanding gained in the previous sections. It also shows why and how food products are developed for particular needs.

In this chapter you will:

★ learn that we all have different needs for food products

★ learn about how nutritional needs vary throughout life.

If we all looked the same, did the same thing at the same time, wore the same clothes, watched the same TV programmes and ate the same food, life would be very boring. Can you imagine eating only mashed potato for every meal?

There are thousands of food products available for us to buy because people choose to eat different things and they need different kinds of food. Their different needs are as follows.

- Nutritional needs: people have different needs as they grow and get older. They also have different needs according to the job they do, the make-up of their body, and any inherited preferences they have.
- Financial and lifestyle needs: people have varying amounts of money to spend on food. Some people choose to spend small or large amounts of their income on food. Some have time to prepare a meal, while others want a ready meal they just have to microwave. Some people want to snack on foods, while others prefer to sit down to a three-course meal.
- Moral and ethical needs: some people choose to be vegetarian or to eat only organic foods because they believe it is better for them and the environment. Their religion might ask them to not eat certain foods such as beef or pork.
- Availability: food products have to be available in the shops before people can buy them. Some foods are available only during the season in which they are naturally grown, or are more expensive out of season.

If you understand these needs by finding out more about them, you will be able to design food products for a particular need such as a low-cost shepherd's pie, a vegetarian curry, or a child's pasta dish.

Nutritional needs

This section looks at the different nutritional needs through life. You will learn more about children's needs and other special needs in the next three chapters.

The following people need to eat a balanced **diet** but their needs change as they grow older.

Harry is three-and-a-half years old. He needs:
- small portions, nicely presented so that they appeal to him
- a variety of foods so that he gets all the nutrients to grow and develop, and to encourage good eating habits
- not too many sugary, salty and fatty snacks, but not a low-fat or high-fibre diet either, as he needs other nutrients to grow and develop.

Talika is fourteen years old. She needs:
- more food than adults for her higher energy needs, as she is growing and very active
- more iron (especially for girls), calcium (for bone growth), vitamins and minerals
- to avoid eating too many snacks that are high in sugar and fat. Teenagers often snack on fatty, sugar-filled foods rather than eat three large meals a day.

Michelle is expecting her first baby in two months' time. She needs:
- slightly more protein and overall more food for energy, but not to 'eat for two'
- enough iron, calcium and vitamin D to help the baby grow
- plenty of NSP (dietary fibre) to prevent constipation.
- enough folic acid for the growth of nerves in the baby. This is actually more important before conception and in the first few months of pregnancy when these important cells will be formed.

Graham is 40 years old. He needs:
- to watch his energy intake because his body has stopped growing and is slowing down a little. He also does not do much exercise
- a good, balanced diet with enough fibre, starch, vitamins and minerals to keep his body functioning properly.

Margaret is 74 years old. She needs:
- less energy foods, such as fats and carbohydrates, as she is likely to be less active
- enough protein as her cells still need repairing
- enough iron, calcium and vitamin D for all other body functions
- enough fluid and fibre to help prevent constipation.

Activity

Design a colourful and informative poster to show the food needs of one of the people described in this chapter. You could cut and paste pictures from the Internet or magazines, or draw your own.

Summary

★ Food manufacturers produce food products for **target groups** – people with particular needs or choices.

Food choices and needs

Children's food needs

In this chapter you will:

★ learn more about children's food needs.

Children need to eat a healthy, balanced **diet** so that they grow and develop, and to avoid health problems in later life. Poor eating habits from a young age are difficult to change later in life. Children need:

• a good balance of nutrients from a wide range of food. A healthy diet means that children are less likely to become overweight as adults and will grow properly

• to be encouraged to eat lots of different foods so they get used to different tastes and textures

• snacks between meals as their appetites are small. These should not be too sugary or fatty

• to limit the amount of fibre-rich food as this can be very filling and means that they may not be able to eat enough food for energy and other nutrients they need

• to eat as a family but have attractive food for children and small portions – eating should be fun

• to drink full-fat milk until the age of five because of the extra nutrients it provides (vitamins A and D, and fat)

• to avoid drinking too many sugary drinks, including natural fruit juices that can rot the teeth

• to avoid eating salty foods. Many processed foods, including ready meals, sausages, burgers and pizzas, should be avoided by the very young as their kidneys cannot cope with salt.

Food products for children

Many food products aimed at children are available in the shops such as dinosaur shaped turkey pieces, alphabet potato shapes and teddy bear chocolate biscuits. However, these can be high in fat, sugar and salt, as well as containing **additives**. More and more young children are becoming seriously overweight. This is caused by a lack of exercise and a diet overloaded with ready-prepared and 'junk' food. Busy parents sometimes prefer to buy ready meals suitable for their children, but they want to know that the nutritional content is good.

Case Study

Loved by Kids

Marks & Spencer has a special range, called Loved by Kids, of ready meals, desserts and snack products aimed at the needs of children. The company has worked with nutritionists to develop the range, so the levels of fat, salt and sugar are controlled and present in the right amounts. The range also contains no artificial colours, flavours or preservatives as some parents are concerned about the effect on children of additives.

The photo shows two of the meals available in the range. The ravioli is served with 'hidden' vegetables in the tomato sauce – puréed vegetables, such as peas and carrots, are disguised in the sauce. The chicken and vegetable pie is presented attractively to appeal to young children.

Two products from the Loved by Kids range

Baby and toddler foods also need to have a good nutritional content with just natural ingredients. More and more of these foods are becoming organic. The labels also often show that no processed sugar, salt, thickeners, processing aids and unnecessary fillers are used to produce these products. Organix is one such range that does this.

Fortified foods

In the UK, half the breakfast cereals available are fortified with extra nutrients, many of them aimed at children. Fortified foods are smart foods. This means they have been changed so that they behave in a special way needed in a particular product.

In the past, fortification was used to prevent or treat a nutrient deficiency or illness such as iodine being added to salt to prevent goitre or vitamin D to milk to prevent rickets. This is still essential in less economically developed countries. White flour is fortified with the vitamins and minerals lost during the milling process – those that are found in a whole wheat grain such as some of the vitamin B's. Margarine is fortified with the vitamins and minerals found in butter. Today, fortified foods are also being used to optimise health – extra nutrients that **consumers** believe are good for them are added to food products.

In the UK, breakfast cereals are fortified the most – many of them contain a variety of added vitamins and minerals. Soft drinks, often those aimed at children, are the next category, followed by milk, biscuits and cereal bars.

It is not only parents who are concerned about a balanced nutritional diet. If you see a food product that says it is fortified with calcium or vitamin C, for example, you may think it must be good for you. However, many fortified foods are also high in fat, salt and sugar. The fact that foods are fortified may mislead some people into thinking they are 'healthier' than they actually are.

Case Study

Micro-encapsulation

Micro-encapsulation has made it possible to fortify foods with different nutrients. For example, Omega Zone cereal bars contain fish oils that have the essential fatty acid Omega 3. This oil is surrounded by a protein-based capsule to hide the smell and taste of the oil. These capsules are tiny and can be seen only under a microscope.

Some probiotic yoghurts use micro-encapsulation. The good bacteria are encapsulated so that they survive the acid conditions of the stomach and can be used in the gut to aid digestion.

Activity

Imagine a food manufacturer has asked you to design a new spaghetti bolognese sauce to appeal to young children. How could you improve the nutritional value of a basic bolognese sauce to make it suitable for children?

A selection of fortified foods

Summary

★ Children have specific dietary needs.

★ The nutritional content of food products for children is important so that they do not become overweight and can develop properly.

★ Some foods are smart foods because they are fortified with extra nutrients.

Food choices and needs

> **In this chapter you will:**
> ★ **learn why food products must be designed with a good nutritional profile.**

Millions of pounds are spent each year by the UK government on trying to improve the nation's health. There are many illnesses where poor **diet** is a major contributing factor.

- **Coronary heart disease** is more likely to happen to people who are overweight and who have too much saturated fat in their diet. The fats from animal sources are saturated fats that the liver makes into cholesterol. High blood cholesterol is a major risk factor in the development of heart disease. Too much fat in the diet often means that it is not used for energy but stored in the body. Being overweight means that there is more strain on the heart.
- **Strokes** are a type of brain injury caused by high blood pressure. Too much salt in the diet is one of the causes of high blood pressure.
- **Diabetes** occurs when the body cannot break down sugars into glucose for energy. Three-quarters of people with diabetes have Type 2 diabetes, which usually occurs in middle or old age. If you are overweight, you are twice as likely to get diabetes. Therefore, a high-sugar and high-fat diet should be avoided.
- **Osteoporosis** is a bone disease that is associated with a lack of calcium in the diet – often from childhood and adolescence, even though the symptoms do not appear until middle to old age. People must build up good bone density in early life so that they do not get this condition. Every three minutes someone fractures a bone because of osteoporosis. One in every three women over the age of 50 has osteoporosis.
- **Diverticulitis** is where the intestine becomes inflamed because waste products are trapped in the muscle wall. It is caused by a lack of NSP (dietary fibre) in the diet. Half of people over the age of 60 in the USA have diverticulosis (stretched intestine), which can lead to diverticulitis. This illness does not occur in people who eat an unprocessed, high-fibre diet.
- **Colon cancer** is not necessarily caused by a poor diet, but it has been suggested that people who eat a diet full

of fruit and vegetables, and other high-fibre foods, are less likely to get this type of cancer.

Five a day

The government recommends an intake of at least five portions of fruit and vegetables a day to help reduce the risk of some cancers, heart disease and other chronic conditions.

1 medium apple 2 broccoli florets 2 halves of canned peaches

1 handful of grapes 1 medium banana 3 heaped tablespoons of peas

1 medium glass of orange juice 7 strawberries 3 whole dried apricots

5 A DAY
Just Eat More
(fruit & veg)
www.doh.gov.uk/fiveaday

3 heaped tablespoons of cooked kidney beans 16 okra NHS

The government recommends we eat at least five portions of fruit and vegetables a day

What is a portion?

Fruit
- One medium apple, pear, banana, and so on.
- A handful of grapes, strawberries, cherries, and so on.
- A small glass of juice
- Four tablespoons of dried fruit

Vegetables
- A large tomato, half a cucumber
- A small plate of salad
- Two large spoons of carrot, cabbage, peas, and so on.

Fruit and vegetables provide many vitamins and minerals that are important for health. These include antioxidants, which may help to maintain a healthy heart. Fruit and vegetables are also high in fibre, low in fat and low in calories.

Salt

Three-quarters of the salt in our diet comes from processed foods; the rest is what we put onto our foods and what is naturally found in foods. Therefore, a diet that includes a lot of processed foods can easily exceed the government guidelines of 6g a day. In a survey of ready meals, one supermarket-brand shepherd's pie was found to contain 6g of salt – the recommended daily maximum.

People often get confused between salt and sodium. Information on sodium is provided on a food label, but this label may not show the amount of salt. Some people do not link the sodium content of food to the salt content. Some food manufacturers are starting to provide the salt content.

Some food manufacturers produce reduced salt products and low-fat products

Fat

Fat is a concentrated source of energy that does not fill you up, so it is easy to eat too many high-fat foods. High-fat diets can make people overweight, causing other medical problems. Most people get too much of their energy from fat. Government recommendations are that we should be eating no more than 75–95 g of fat a day, depending on

age, gender and weight. This can be difficult if we look at the fat content of some everyday foods.

Food product	Fat content (%)
Vegetable oil	100
Butter	82
Cheddar cheese	34
Pork sausages	32
Minced beef	16

You can see that eating a lasagne made with minced beef and a cheese sauce can mean eating a very fatty meal. To help reduce the amount of fat in our diet, some food manufacturers have introduced low-fat ranges of food products containing less than 3% fat.

Nutritional claims

If a food or drink label says it is:

- reduced fat, it must contain at least 25% less fat than the standard range
- less than 5% fat, it must contain no more than 5g of fat per 100g of food or drink
- low fat, it must contain no more than 3g of fat per 100g of food or drink.

Activities

1 Make a standard mousse and adapt the recipe to make a low-fat version. Use a nutritional analysis program to compare the results. What differences do you notice?

2 A **specification** for a pasta product requires it to have three vegetables included. Find a recipe for a pasta product and develop it to include three different types of vegetable.

Summary

★ Food products need to be developed to promote a healthy diet.

Food choices and needs

Food allergies

In this chapter you will:

★ learn about particular food ingredients that can cause problems for some people.

More and more food products are being manufactured today for people with food intolerances or allergies. Up to 2% of the population are believed to be intolerant to everyday foods such as milk, eggs, fish and wheat.

A food intolerance is when someone has an unpleasant reaction to a certain food or food ingredient. A food allergy is a type of food intolerance that involves the body's immune system. Symptoms of these allergies and intolerances can be skin rashes, eczema, wind, cramps, poor growth in children, hyperactivity, diarrhoea and anaphylactic shock (where the body's tissues swell up, which can cause death). These allergies and intolerances need to be taken seriously.

Food manufacturers make a variety of products that are targeted at people with allergies or intolerances

Peanut allergy

Peanut allergy is the most commonly known allergy because it often causes the most dramatic symptoms, affecting people's breathing and causing anaphylactic shock. Anaphylactic shock is a serious condition where the throat swells up, preventing air from getting into the lungs. Many bread, cake and biscuit packages say that the product may contain nuts because, although that particular product does not include nuts as an ingredient, the bread, cake or biscuit has been made in the same factory as other products containing nuts. The food industry uses a peanut-testing kit to identify the presence of peanuts in products.

Other allergies

Other allergies include egg, which usually causes rashes and eczema; fish and shellfish, which can also cause anaphylactic shock; and soya, including soya sauce, tofu and textured vegetable protein (TVP), which can cause diarrhoea, vomiting and eczema.

Milk intolerance

This causes abdominal pain, bloating and diarrhoea. There are two main types of reaction to milk. Someone can be allergic to milk protein or they can be intolerant to the lactose (milk sugar) in the milk. People with lactose intolerance do not have the enzyme called lactase in their stomachs, so they cannot digest it. These people can eat cheese and yoghurt because the lactose in these products has been changed to lactic acid.

Coeliac disease and gluten intolerance

As many as one in 300 people in the UK has coeliac disease. These people are unable to eat products made from wheat, barley, rye and possibly oats, as they are sensitive to gluten, the protein found in these cereals. People with this allergy damage the lining of the small intestine if gluten is eaten. This prevents the absorption of nutrients, leading to weight loss and malnutrition. Eating gluten can also cause a skin reaction.

Gluten intolerance produces a less severe reaction. People with a gluten intolerance may suffer from bloating, stomach cramps and diarrhoea.

Many food products are made from wheat such as bread, pasta, cakes, biscuits and pastry. This means that people diagnosed with coeliac disease need to change their **diet**. Food labels have to be checked carefully for 'hidden' wheat products such as those in malt products, breadcrumbs, batters, sauce mixes, couscous (made from wheat), dry-roasted peanuts, semolina, some breakfast cereals, sausages (contains rusk made from wheat), burgers and many others.

Gluten-free products

Gluten free

Gluten-free products are widely available

Gluten-free products use alternative cereals to wheat, barley, rye and oats. There are commercial gluten-free flours on the market. For example, Doves Farm gluten-free plain white flour contains a blend of maize, rice, buckwheat and potato flours. Its gluten-free brown bread flour is made from rice, potato and tapioca flours, together with natural fibre and gums for baking strength. The most difficult thing to make without wheat is bread because the gluten, when it is stretched during the kneading process, creates the texture and forms the structure of the bread.

Doves Farm gluten-free flour

Food manufacturers also experiment with other starches when they make cakes, biscuits, pasta and pastry. These starches include soya flour, rice flour, manioc flour (made from cassava), millet flour, tapioca flour, maize flour, potato flour, buckwheat flour, sorghum flour, quinoa flour and nut flour (especially almond).

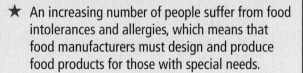

Activities

1 Use sensory analysis to compare gluten-free pasta products with wheat-based pasta products.

2 Use the Internet to find out about gluten-free products. Try the Sainsbury's and Doves Farm websites by going to www.heinemann.co.uk/hotlinks and clicking on this activity.

3 Experiment with different flours to make a gluten-free cake.

? Test your knowledge

1 Explain what 'food intolerance' means, giving examples of some everday foods that some people are intolerent to.

2 What ingredients can producers of gluten-free flour use as an alternative to wheat, barley, rye and oats?

Summary

★ An increasing number of people suffer from food intolerances and allergies, which means that food manufacturers must design and produce food products for those with special needs.

★ It is possible to buy foods that do not contain a whole range of ingredients such as eggs, milk, nuts, soya and yeast.

★ Food manufacturers need to include accurate allergen information on their product labels.

In this chapter you will:
★ learn about the ethical and moral needs of some **consumers**.

As you have already seen from pages 34 and 35, some people do not choose food products just for their nutritional or dietary needs. Some make food choices because of their morals and ethics – what they feel and think is right.

Religious needs

Many religions have dietary rules that affect the choices followers make about the foods they eat. The table below shows some of the rules laid down by six faiths.

Religion	Foods forbidden	Special considerations
Christianity	None	Fish is eaten traditionally on Fridays instead of meat
Islam	Pork, fish without scales, shellfish and alcohol	Food must be halal ('permitted'), which includes a method of slaughtering and preparation according to Muslim law
Hinduism	Beef, alcohol	Cattle are sacred and must not be eaten Most Hindus are vegetarians
Judaism	Pork, fish without scales and shellfish	Food must be kosher ('permitted'), which includes a method of slaughtering and preparation according to Jewish law Orthodox Jews do not eat dairy products with meat, and use separate kitchen utensils to use with dairy or meat foods
Buddhism	None	Buddhism teaches that it is wrong to kill, so many Buddhists are vegetarian
Rastafarianism	None, but Rastas eat food that is considered to be in its natural or whole state	Each individual decides on their own dietary restrictions

Vegetarians

A vegetarian is someone who lives on a **diet** of grains, pulses, nuts, seeds, vegetables and fruits, with or without the use of dairy products and eggs. Vegetarians do not eat meat, poultry, game, fish or shellfish, or slaughter by-products such as gelatine or animal fats.

At least 5% of the UK population are now vegetarian. In the last ten years, the number of vegetarians in the UK has nearly doubled. A third of the population eats meat only occasionally, and two-thirds eat some meatless meals. Sales of vegetarian products are increasing by around 15% each year.

There are several types of vegetarians:
• lacto-ovo-vegetarian: eat both dairy products and eggs. This is the most common type of vegetarian diet
• lacto-vegetarian: eat dairy products but not eggs
• vegans: do not eat dairy products, eggs or any other animal product because they are from animals.

There are also some people who do not eat red meat but do eat fish and poultry.

There are many reasons why people choose to become vegetarian.

Some people become vegetarian for ethical reasons:
• they believe it is wrong to slaughter animals for food
• they are opposed to cruelty and suffering inflicted on animals reared for food
• they are concerned about the environment, believing meat production to be non-economic. The land used to produce 1kg of meat can produce 200kg of tomatoes, 160kg of potatoes, and 80kg of apples.

Others believe there are health advantages to a vegetarian diet.
• they believe that a vegetarian diet is more healthy, low in saturated fat and high in starch, dietary fibre, vitamins and minerals
• some groups keep to a vegetarian diet for religious reasons.

Foods suitable for vegetarians

There is no single legal definition of the word 'vegetarian' in the UK. This means that there is no one set of rules about when a food can be called vegetarian. Manufacturers are not required by law to label foods as being suitable for vegetarians – it is a voluntary practice. Food approved by the Vegetarian Society can display the society's logo. Other symbols are used by different manufacturers.

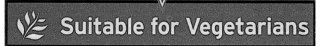

Some food manufacturers use logos to identify vegetarian food products

There is a campaign called 'NOVA', which is trying to get a compulsory global system for labelling all food products. This is promoted as a clear and comprehensive system, which ethically covers all aspects of a product's contents and origin. It stands for:

- N shows that the product is natural, either that it has not been genetically modified or that it contains no artificial or chemical additives.
- O shows that the product is 100% organic and produced with no chemical pesticides or fertilisers.
- V shows vegetarian suitability on all products.
- A shows that the product has not been tested on animals.

Therefore, all products would contain some or all of these elements.

People do not have to be religious or vegetarian to choose foods for moral and ethical reasons. The NOVA campaign shows that some people prefer organic products or that they want to know that they are not eating genetically modified foods. Increasing numbers of people are concerned about where their food comes from: where it is grown, how it is grown, who grows it and when it is grown.

? Test your knowledge

1 Name two religious groups that follow a vegetarian diet. In each case, explain what foods they avoid.

2 Why would some people avoid eating the following foods?
- Ham sandwich
- Bacon and eggs
- Fish fried in dripping

3 Which of the following foods would the Vegetarian Society be happy to approve?

INGREDIENTS: Glucose Syrup, Sugar, Water, Gelatine, Acetic Acid, Acidity Regulator: Sodium Citrates, Flavouring, Citric Acid, Lemon Juice, Colour: Carmoisine, Raspberry Juice.

er 100g as sold 296kcal 4.4g 69.6g 0g 0g Fat

A

Per scone	243 Calories	9.3g Fat

Ingredients: Wheat Flour, Water, Golden Sultanas (11%) (Preservative: Sulphur Dioxide), Butter (11%), Sultanas (9%), Light Brown Sugar, Sugar, Liquid Egg, Whole Milk Powder, Raising Agents: Disodium Dihydrogen Diphosphate, Sodium Hydrogen Carbonate; Invert Sugar Syrup, Egg Powder, Salt.

B

Per pie	535 Calories	30.0g Fat

Ingredients
Wheat Flour, Beef Steak (31%), Water, Margarine (Vegetable Oil and Hydrogenated Vegetable Oil (Rapeseed and Palm), Water, Salt, Emulsifier: Mono- and Diglycerides of Fatty Acid), Shortening (Vegetable Oil (Rapeseed), Emulsifier: Mono- and Diglycerides of Fatty Acid), Onions, Lard, Modified Maize Starch, Egg, Beef Fat, Red Wine, Salt, Tomato Puree, Beef Stock (Beef Extract, Beef Stock, Yeast Extract, Salt), Malt Extract, Black Pepper, Acidity Regulator: Monopotassium Tartrate.

C

Summary

★ Food manufacturers must consider a growing trend in ethical and moral needs when designing food products.

Sourcing ingredients

In this chapter you will:

★ learn to understand the broader issues, such as social and economic implications, associated with food production.

Food miles

A food mile is the distance a food travels from where it has grown to where it is eaten. Supermarkets and food manufacturers buy food from all over the world to make into food products or to sell as raw food such as fruit, vegetables and meat. Does it matter if many of these ingredients have travelled hundreds of food miles before they are available in the shops?

The ingredients of a traditional Christmas lunch bought from a supermarket may have travelled thousands of miles. The poultry could have been imported from Thailand and travelled nearly 11,000 miles. The runner beans may have come from Zambia (4500 miles), the carrots from Spain (1000 miles), the potatoes from Italy (1500 miles) and the sprouts from the UK, where they were transported around the country before reaching the shop (125 miles). By the time trucking to and from warehouses to stores is added, the total distance the food has travelled may be over 20,000 miles, or the equivalent of travelling around the world once. Think of the costs involved, not only of the fuel. The environmental costs are also high, with pollution from emissions (gases produced by vehicles, which damage the environment) and traffic jams.

If **consumers** and food manufacturers choose seasonal products and purchase them locally, such as from farm shops and markets, the food miles of the traditional Christmas lunch could be greatly reduced. The cost of transport would be reduced as less fuel is used, and fewer harmful emissions would be given off from vehicles.

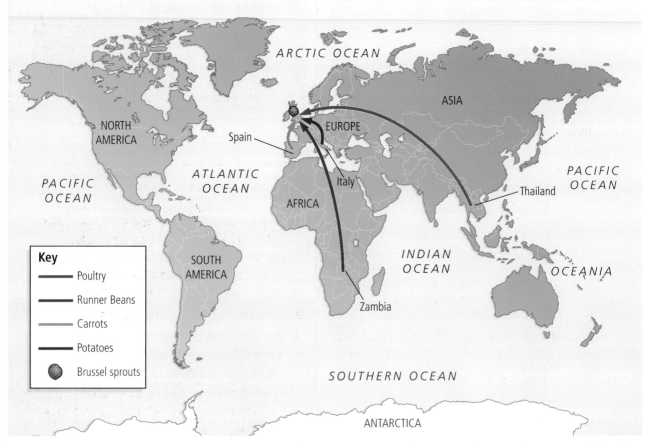

Many everyday ingredients may have travelled hundreds of miles before they reach the plate

Resources

The reason food miles matter is because transporting foods long distances means using more oil, which is a non-renewable resource. At some stage in the future, oil supplies will run out. No matter how the food is transported – by air, sea, train or road – oil is used. Intensive methods of production mean that, on average, people are using ten calories of energy input (oil) for one calorie of food produced. This energy input is used to heat greenhouses, make fertilisers and pesticides, and pump water to crops.

Provenance

Organic food uses less energy during production because no chemical fertilisers or pesticides are used, but it may nevertheless travel many food miles before arriving at its final destination.

The provenance of food is becoming more and more important. Provenance means where the food has been made or grown, who has made it, how it has been made and when it was made. More and more manufacturers have ethical or responsible trading policies that govern where and how foods have been made or grown.

In Lancashire, a group of fifteen farmers in the small area of the Forest of Bowland have set up a co-operative so that their milk is bottled locally and then sold locally in supermarkets. Consumers know the farms this milk is produced on and that very few food miles have been used to get it to the shop. The slogan of this co-operative is 'Faster from pasture to you'.

Seasonal food

One way to cut down on food miles is to eat locally sourced, seasonal foods. The problem is that it can be confusing in a supermarket where food is bought from all over the world. For example, apples are always in season somewhere in the world, so it is important to read the labels carefully and buy foods produced in the UK where possible.

Case Study

New Covent Garden Food Co.

This company uses all natural ingredients, with no **additives**, preservatives or colourings, sourced from farmers and growers who care about the food they produce. They produce a range of seasonal soups:

'Fresh ingredients vary with the season. Using in-season ingredients is a logical, least wasteful and most natural way to cook. It provides us with ingredients that are plentiful when they're at their natural best.'

Activities

1   Carry out some research at your local supermarkets and shops to find out where some of the foods available have come from. Present your findings in a table, calculating the food miles of each product if possible. Which item has travelled furthest?

2   Design and make a seasonal soup or salad.

Summary

★ It is important to consider wider moral, social, cultural and environmental implications when designing food products.

Food choices and needs

> **In this chapter you will:**
> ★ learn to consider historical and cultural factors when developing products.

In the UK, we live in a multicultural society, with many families having origins from other parts of the world such as India, China, Africa and the Caribbean. Other families have originated from countries in Europe such as Poland, Italy and Portugal. The food we eat has been influenced by these cultures.

Cheap air travel has also had an effect on the food we eat. More and more of us travel abroad for holidays. We arrive back wanting to eat some of the delicious food we have eaten abroad such as paella and moussaka.

If you ask older people born in the UK about the foods they ate as children, you would see that they ate traditional British foods such as fish and chips, roasts, pies and puddings rather than spaghetti bolognese from Italy and curry from India.

Many traditional foods in the UK have a regional flavour. Dishes that are now eaten across the country have often originated from and are associated with a particular place. Yorkshire pudding, haggis, Cheddar cheese and Lancashire hotpot are some examples. These regional

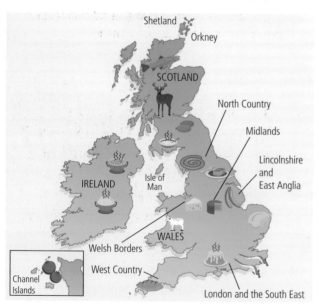

Regional foods are now available countrywide

foods are becoming more popular with **consumers**. Some restaurants serve regional specialities on their menus.

Black pudding

Bury market's black pudding stall

Black pudding is a regional dish that has a long history in Britain. It has traditionally been eaten for breakfast. It is perhaps the most ancient of sausages or puddings. The reason for its long history is simple. When a pig was killed, there was a lot of blood. This blood did not keep fresh for long, so mixing it together with offal (liver, heart and kidneys) into a casing and cooking it was an obvious solution. Some puddings were often dried to make them last longer.

Black pudding – which is called different names in other countries such as boudin noir, blutwurst or morcilla – is eaten by many Europeans. In the UK, black pudding is now eaten mostly in the north. The county of Lancashire lays claim to the best black puddings and the town of Bury to the very best of those. There is a stall on the open market in Bury that sells only black puddings, lean or fatty. You can buy them to take home ready for breakfast or supper, and you can also buy them as a hot snack. There are many butchers in the north of the UK who make their own black puddings. They each have a secret recipe with different mixes of herbs and spices. Other ingredients often include oatmeal, flour, barley, other offal, onion and fat.

Case Study

Two Lancashire chefs

Two award-winning Lancashire chefs include black pudding as one of their 'signature dishes' (the few dishes they are well known for).

Nigel Howarth from the Northcote Manor has created a starter of black pudding with smoked trout mousse and a mustard sauce. Paul Heathcote of Heathcotes has created a starter of black pudding on crushed potatoes and baked beans with a bay leaf sauce.

These two chefs, together with other chefs from the region, have elevated this traditional basic food to make it a respectable thing to eat.

Nigel Howarth's black pudding

Paul Heathcote's black pudding

Cultural foods

McDonald's restaurants are found all over the world, and you might think that the menu is the same in every restaurant. However, different cultures want to eat different foods. In India, a large percentage of the population are vegetarian, so the McDonald's menu includes a range of specially developed pure vegetarian food – even the mayonnaise is made without eggs. Items include McAloo Tikki Burger and McCurry Veg.

The cooking area for vegetarian products is separated from the other sections of the kitchen, and separate equipment is used for cooking them. Members of staff cooking vegetarian foods wear green aprons to identify them.

The menu also reflects the traditional foods and tastes of India. It includes Indian-style seasoning and spices, and does not include beef as many Indians are Hindu and do not eat beef because the cow is considered sacred.

Activities

1 Use the Internet or books on local life to research a local regional food. Explain its origins and how it is made.

2 Research a regional dish and develop it into a healthier option.

3 Use the Internet to compare menus at two restaurants, one in Scotland and the other in southern England. What differences do you notice?

Summary

★ Historical and cultural factors need to be considered in the development of food products.

★ Retailers sell different kinds of food products in different parts of the UK.

★ The location of the supermarket, shop or restaurant may affect what people want to buy.

Food choices and needs

Recipe engineering

In this chapter you will:

★ understand why and how food manufacturers design food products for their needs.

Food manufacturers design food products to fit the specific needs of the **consumer** such as nutritional, moral, ethical and financial. They also target other needs such as:

- it can be cooked quickly
- it is easy to eat
- it looks and tastes good
- it is trendy.

Food manufacturers target consumer needs – the cheesecake is visually attractive while the two microwave meals can be cooked very quickly

Food manufacturers must also consider their needs. They must be able to produce the food product in large quantities, so the process must be simple to complete using machinery. They must be able to sell it and make a **profit**, so the product needs a good **shelf life** and reasonably priced ingredients.

Recipe engineering

Food manufacturers use standard recipes for food products (see pages 72 and 73). These are basic recipes for products that can then be adapted. Food manufacturers then engineer them to suit different needs.

Large-scale production

Manufacturers need to scale-up the recipe so that hundreds of portions can be made at one time. They do this so that the proportions of the ingredients remain the same. The table below shows a recipe for egg custard tart that has been scaled-up for large-scale production.

	Small-scale/prototype	Large-scale
Pastry		
Flour	200 g	100 kg
Vegetable fat/lard	50 g	25 kg
Margarine/butter	50 g	25 kg
Water	2–3 tablespoons	15 litres
Caster sugar	25 g	12.5 kg
Egg	1 yolk	14 kg whole egg
Salt	1 pinch	500 g
Dextrose	–	500 g
Filling		
Eggs	$2\frac{1}{2}$	100 kg
Caster sugar	50 g	25 kg
Milk	500 ml	32 kg
Vanilla essence	2–3 drops	500 ml
Grated nutmeg	tsp	1 kg
Colouring	–	50 ml

They also may need to change some of the ingredients. For example, instead of solid fat, oil might be used because it is easier to move around the factory. Solid fat would have to be manually placed in the mixer, whereas oil can be piped into the mixing vats. Other ingredients might take too long to prepare, such as fresh mushrooms, or they might be difficult to handle in large quantities such as strawberries and other soft fruit.

Oil is transported from storage vats into food mixers along pipes

LARGE PORK PIE

FREEZING   Not suitable for home freezing

INGREDIENTS Wheat Flour, Pork (27%), Pork Fat, Lard, Water, Rusk, Salt, Pork Gelatine, Wheat Starch, Wheat Protein, Pepper, Potato Starch, Flavour Enhancer: Monosodium Glutamate, Casein.

NUTRITIONAL

INGREDIENTS

RUSK, DRIED ONIONS, VEGETABLE SUET (VEGETABLE AND HYDROGENATED VEGETABLE OILS, WHEATFLOUR), DRIED PARSLEY (1.4%), DRIED THYME (1%), LEMON FLAVOURING (LEMON OIL, CITRIC ACID, ANTIOXIDANT: BUTYLATED HYDROXYANISOLE; DEXTRINS), DRIED BASIL, SPICES, DRIED LEMON PEEL (0.1%).

Cheaper ingredients such as rusk are often added to bulk up the finished product

Manufacturers also need to add extra ingredients because the process is different for large-scale production. For example, adding glycerine improves the moisture of a cake mixture; adding dextrose to pastry gives a light brown colour when baked.

They may also need to add **additives** to increase the shelf life of the product and make it the right colour, flavour and texture.

Changing ingredients for cost

Manufacturers must produce food products at an acceptable price for consumers so they will buy the product. They need to think carefully about the cost of ingredients and experiment with proportions for a good price as well as taste. They must consider the use of bulk ingredients. These are inexpensive ingredients that increase easily the volume or bulk of a final product.

- Breadcrumbs or rusk are used in sausages, burgers, stuffing and puddings. They absorb flavours and liquid and help bind ingredients together.
- Potatoes and other vegetables such as pulses are used in a variety of savoury products like pasties, soups and casseroles so that not too much meat or fish is used because these are more expensive.
- Textured vegetable protein (TVP) is much cheaper than meat and can be added in different ratios to meat-based products.
- Water is added to products so that the quantities of more expensive ingredients, such as meat, are reduced.

Therefore, food manufacturers carry out recipe engineering to:
- make it suitable for large-scale production
- make it cheaper to manufacture
- make it last longer, look better and taste better.

They might also use recipe engineering to:
- change its nutritional profile
- make it an ethical product such as vegetarian, organic, GM-free.

Activities

1   Compare the ingredients of three different strawberry jams from a wide price range. What is the heaviest ingredient in each one?

2   Look at this list of ingredients from a packet of scones. Compare the ingredients with those you would use to make scones. Explain why these different ingredients are used.

Devon Scones

This pack contains 6 Devon Scones

INGREDIENTS

Wheatflour, Sugar, Vegetable & Hydrogenated Vegetable Oil, Water, Vegetable Glycerine, Full Cream, Milk Powder, Whole Egg, Raising Agents: Disodium Diphosphate, Sodium Hydrogen Carbonate; Salt

Summary

★ Food manufacturers also have needs when they produce food products.

Food choices and needs

In this chapter you will:

★ understand why **additives** are used in some food products.

Additives are synthetic or natural substances, added in small quantities to food during processing. They are used to give additional quality to some processed foods.

Additives are used to:

- improve or enhance the flavour, aroma or appearance of foods
- help the processing and preparation of food and ensure consistent quality; for example, the use of anti-foaming agents to reduce foaming in jam-making or the addition of emulsifiers to stabilise salad cream
- prevent food spoilage and prolong **shelf life**. Preservatives are additives and they are added to bread and other baked products to make them last longer
- produce quick, easy, convenient foods such as Pot Noodle, instant whipped desserts and instant potato mash
- restore the original characteristics of a food after processing; for example, putting the green back into tinned processed peas
- produce a bigger variety of food products; for example, a range of potato crisps with different flavours such as prawn cocktail, smoky bacon and barbecue
- maintain or increase the nutritional value of foods.

There are over 300 listed additives and more than 3000 flavourings. Some of these have been used for many years. As food science and technology has developed, a wider range of chemicals has started to be used in foods during their processing.

Additives have to be approved by the Government Food Advisory Committee. Long, strict tests are carried out to check for unwanted effects before approval is given. On approval, each additive is given a number as a means of identification in Europe. These are called **E numbers**, which means that it is accepted for use throughout the European Union.

Additives and their functions

There are several categories of additives used in food products.

- Flavours and flavour enhancers: these can be natural, such as herbs and spices, natural identical (made in a laboratory but chemically the same as the natural product) or artificial (man-made and not found in nature).
- Colours: E numbers E100–E199. These restore colour lost during processing or make food more colourful. They can be natural, natural identical or artificial.

Many processed foods contain additives

- Preservatives: E numbers E200–E299. These increase storage life by preventing the growth of bacteria. Some of these have been used since the times of the Ancient Romans and Greeks, and are important ingredients in certain traditional foods.
- Antioxidants: E numbers E300–E321. These prevent food containing fat from going bad. They prevent oxidisation of fruit and vegetables and extend shelf life.
- Emulsifiers and stabilisers: E numbers E322–E499. These improve the consistency of food during processing and storage. They are used to help substances such as oil and water to mix together, form an emulsion and stay mixed. They give foods a smooth, creamy texture and lengthen the shelf life of some products. Lecithin, a natural emulsion in eggs, is used to make mayonnaise (see pages 96 and 97). It also occurs in soya beans.

E numbers above 500 are given to sweeteners, acids, anti-caking agents, anti-foaming agents, bulking agents, flour improvers, glazing agents, humectants (which attract water), modified starch, propellants (used in sprays such as cream aerosols), packaging gases, raising agents and other categories.

The addition of nutrients to fortify food products has been looked at on pages 110 and 111.

Do we really need additives?

Food additives are causing behavioural problems in an entire generation of youngsters, an alarming government-backed study confirms today.

Burton's Foods say they are changing the recipe for its popular Jammie Dodger biscuits because of **consumer** concerns. From September 2004 the jam in the centre will be less red. The firm will stop using carmoisine (E122), which will be replaced by a more natural version.

More and more consumers want to buy 'natural' food products because of their concerns about additives. They do not like the thought of chemicals being added to their food. Some think that additives may cause allergies, asthma and hyperactivity in children. Others think additives are unnecessary and are just added for extra colour and flavour. In some cases, they might be added to hide or disguise lower quality ingredients. Even though additives are tested thoroughly before being approved, it is not always possible to know the long-term effects of eating them.

Consumers often choose organic foods because they know that they will be additive free. There will be no additives listed on the ingredients label. The consumer can also be reassured that there have been no hidden additives acquired during the growing, processing and packaging of the food. For example, organic meat will not contain growth hormones or antibiotic residues. Organic baby and children's food are becoming particularly popular. Thirty per cent of the baby food market is now organic.

Manufacturers want to meet these consumer demands but the use of less additives can often mean a shorter shelf life. This would mean the food would cost more to produce. Manufacturers are also concerned that certain foods would not sell because of the appearance of the food when it has no additives.

? Test your knowledge

1. Most baby food manufacturers claim that their foods are free from artificial additives. Why are some parents likely to buy these foods?
2. Explain the advantages and disadvantages of using additives in foods.

Summary

★ Food manufacturers use a wide range of additives during the food processing for many reasons.

★ Some consumers prefer food products made without additives.

Food choices and needs

Adapting recipes for different needs

In this chapter you will:

★ look at examples of ways to adapt products to help with your own design decisions.

Pages 122 and 123 have shown how and why changes to standard recipes take place. Let's look at two examples of some of the ways two dishes – shepherd's pie and macaroni cheese – can be adapted to suit the needs of different groups of people. This should give you ideas on how to adapt other dishes.

Looking at examples of how to make design changes will help you with your own work. All the chapters in this section have shown different needs of **consumers** and manufacturers.

Shepherd's pie

Ethical needs:
- Use organic beef, vegetables and milk.
- Use locally sourced products.

Healthy option (reduced fat):
- Use lean meat for the filling.
- Do not add fat – the onions could be dry fried.
- Do not add butter to the mashed potato.
- Use skimmed milk in the mashed potato.

Children:
- Make small portions (children's appetites are small).
- Present a smiley face on the mashed potato, with colour added to the mash using carrots (to appeal to children).
- Add hidden vegetables to the meat filling such as puréed peas, tomato and carrots (to provide essential nutrients for growing children).

Gluten-free:
- Do not use wheat flour to thicken the meat filling.
- Remember that ready-manufactured stocks often contain wheat flour.

Pregnant women:
- Add vegetables high in folic acid such as broccoli.

Basic shepherd's pie

Children's version

Pregnant woman's version

A basic shepherd's pie can be adapted easily to meet different needs

Basic ingredients

Topping:		Filling:	
	200g potato		50g onion
	25ml milk		250g minced meat
	10g butter		115ml oil
			25g flour
			100ml stock
			Seasoning

Vegetarian/vegan:
- Do not use meat.
- Use meat analogues such as Quorn or TVP.
- Use alternative proteins such as beans and lentils; use a mixture of these for high biological value.
- Use vegetable oil for frying.
- Do not use butter or milk in the mashed potato if dish is for vegans – use soya milk.

Lower cost:
- Use TVP instead of meat or a combination of TVP and meat such as 40% TVP and 60% meat.
- Bulk out the dish with other cheaper ingredients such as pulses and vegetables.
- Change the proportion of the meat filling and the mashed potato topping to have a thinner layer of meat and a thicker layer of potato.
- Make the portion sizes smaller.

Manufacturing (the **component** parts to this dish are easy to make in large quantities, both in preparation and assembly):
- Use a computerised depositor to place the meat filling into the container.
- Use robotics to pipe the mashed potato on the top.
- Use special packaging to extend the **shelf life**.

Macaroni cheese

Children:
- Make small portions.
- Use special shaped pasta such as alphabet pasta.
- Use mild cheese in the sauce to match children's tastes.
- Add vegetables to the cheese sauce for colour and nutrition such as sweetcorn and peas.

Pregnant women:
- Add vegetables high in folic acid such as broccoli.

Manufacturing (the component parts to this dish are easy to make in large quantities, both in preparation and assembly):
- Use a computerised depositor to place the pasta and sauce into the container.
- Use a smart (modified) starch in the sauce to maintain the quality of the sauce when it is chilled or frozen.

Lower cost:
- Reduce the quantity of cheese used and use monosodium glutamate, an additive, as a flavour enhancer.
- Change the proportion of cheese sauce to pasta, to have less sauce and more pasta.
- Make the portion sizes smaller.

Basic macaroni cheese

Pregnant woman's version   *Children's version*

A basic macaroni cheese can be adapted easily to meet different needs

Basic ingredients

100g pasta
300ml milk
25g butter
25g flour
100g cheese
Seasoning

Vegan:
- Use vegan cheese.
- Use vegetable fat.
- Use soya milk.

Ethical needs:
- Use organic cheese and milk.
- Use locally sourced products.

Gluten-free:
- Do not use wheat flour to thicken the cheese sauce.
- Use wheat-free pasta.

Healthy option (reduced fat):
- Reduce the quantity of cheese used.
- Use low-fat cheese.
- Do not add fat to the sauce.
- Use skimmed milk in the sauce.

Activity

Use the examples on these pages to show how you could adapt a chicken curry.

Summary

★ Adapting a standard recipe for a particular need is a simple process once you have information about the need of the consumer and the manufacturer, and a knowledge of the function of ingredients, proportions and ratios.

Food choices and needs

Exam questions

1 People choose to eat a variety of different food products.

a A food manufacturer is keen to develop a range of vegetarian products. Explain why this would be popular with consumers. *(6 marks)*

b Food technologists have manufactured alternative protein foods to take the place of meat.

i Give two examples of manufactured alternative protein foods. *(2 marks)*

ii Describe what each is made from. *(4 marks)*

iii Explain how they can be used in food products. *(2 Marks)*

Example of manufactured alternative protein foods	What is each made from?	How can they be used?
1		
2		

c Explain how these proteins will improve the nutritional profile of food products. *(4 marks)*

(AQA/NEAB 2000)

2 Part of a label from the packaging of chicken and prawn parcels is shown below.

Chicken and Prawn Parcels	
Ingredients	
Prawn, Chicken, Pastry, (Wheat flour, Butter, Water, Salt, Raising Agent) Water Chestnuts, Vegetable Oil, Bamboo Shoot Puree, Sesame Oil, Potato Starch, Sugar, Spring Onion. Flavour Enhancer: Monosodium Glutamate, Salt Pepper.	
	Not suitable for vegetarians

a Explain in detail why this product is not suitable for a vegetarian. *(4 marks)*

b Explain how the list of ingredients can be modified to make this product suitable for a vegetarian. *(4 marks)*

(AQA/NEAB 2002)

3 Labelling must inform the consumer of any additives. Food manufacturers are allowed to add safe substances to foods if they are needed.

a List five reasons for using additives. *(5 marks)*

b What does the E in front of a number mean? *(2 marks)*

c Why is it important for the manufacturer to tell the consumer if a product contains nuts? *(2 marks)*

(AQA/NEAB 1999)

4 Mayonnaise can be used as a base for dips.

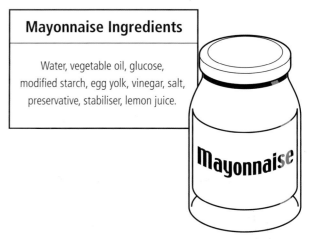

Mayonnaise Ingredients
Water, vegetable oil, glucose, modified starch, egg yolk, vinegar, salt, preservative, stabiliser, lemon juice.

What are the functions of the following ingredients?

Ingredient	Function
Preservative	
Modified starch	

(4 marks)
(AQA 2003)

7 Doing your coursework project

This section covers the steps you must carry out to complete the design process that is your coursework. You should also use other chapters in this book that explain in more detail some of the steps you need to carry out.

You must choose a project outline (design brief) that allows you to design and make food products that could be mass produced and sold. You also need to consider the packaging of the product.

Designing and making food products

Food technology is a practical subject area that requires the application of knowledge and understanding when developing ideas and planning, producing and evaluating products. Designing and making skills are the basis of all your learning in food technology.

Designing and making a food product involves:
★ researching what is already available
★ finding out what people like
★ looking at what ingredients are available
★ understanding how food materials interact together
★ analysing and summarising what you have found out
★ producing an outline specification
★ producing a range of ideas
★ evaluating design ideas and choosing one

★ writing a product specification for that chosen product
★ developing your chosen idea as a prototype
★ considering how the prototype could be manufactured, including:
  • writing a manufacturing specification
  • finding out and producing some of the information that needs to go on the packaging
  • suggesting which materials would be suitable for the packaging
  • identifying the method of production
  • writing a production plan
  • carrying out risk assessments
  • applying quality controls
★ evaluating and testing at every stage of the process
★ matching materials and components with tools, equipment and processes to produce quality products
★ making products singly and in quantity, showing the use of quality controls
★ making quality products suitable for intended users and working out modifications that would improve the quality so that they match the specification.

Time is an important consideration during your coursework and when making products. You could use a chart to help you plan your time effectively.

What's in this section?

7.1 Choosing a project outline and analysing the brief

In this chapter you will:
★ learn how to choose a project outline and analyse it so that you can start the design process.

Coursework is worth 60% of the final GCSE mark. This work has to be planned carefully as only 40 hours are allocated to the full-course coursework. If you are following the short course, 20 hours are allowed for this work. This means you must plan carefully and be clear and focused at each step.

Designing

40% of the coursework marks are allowed for your design work – the work in your folder. This should be around 15 A3 sheets (or 30 A4 sheets) for the full course. If you are following the short course, the amount of work in your folder will be less. Whichever course you are studying, your work should be concise and include only relevant information. For example, you should not include sheets of research printed off the Internet or nutritional data printouts. Marking your coursework is done holistically. This means that it is given an overall mark as a whole piece of work.

Making

60% of the coursework marks are allowed for the practical making activities you carry out. You need to be organised and aim to complete as many making activities as possible. Making means not just making one-off complete products. Making is:
★ experimenting with ingredients
★ modelling parts of a product or making small quantities of a product (prototypes)
★ tasting existing products
★ nutritional analysis of ingredients and recipes
★ computer development and analysis (such as nutritional profiling)
★ comparison testing of shop-bought and homemade products
★ batch production of a food product
★ making one-off products.

Project outline

Your coursework starts with you choosing a project outline, which identifies the types of food products you need to make and who these products are aimed at. You will be given a choice of projects or you will be given time to create your own project outline. To gain higher marks, you will also need to consider how your product would be made on a large scale.

To determine what type of coursework you will carry out:
★ you need to get guidance from your teacher and family
★ you need to choose a project outline that interests you, as your coursework will be carried out over several months
★ you need to choose a project outline that lets you make food products you like making.

Analysis of the project outline

Once you have chosen your project outline, you need to analyse it so that you can work out what you have to do to get started. One way to start analysing is to mind map what each key word means. Example 1 on the opposite page shows this. The project outline for this example is 'Design and make a product that could be sold within a party pack of multicultural foods'. In example 2, for the project outline 'Design and make a celebration cake to be sold in a supermarket retail store', the student has gathered some ideas and identified what kind of research they will need to carry out.

Development of analysis

The next step to take is to develop these words and short sentences into more detailed sentences or bullet points so that it is clear that you understand what to do next. You can refer back to this analysis to check what you have or have not done during the first part of the work.

Your coursework needs to 'tell a story' to someone reading it. A clear analysis of the project outline is the start of this story. Example 2 shows these two steps put together.

Summary
★ You must spend time choosing the right project outline.
★ Analysing the project outline makes you realise what you need to do next and to plan your work.

Example 1: A-grade project

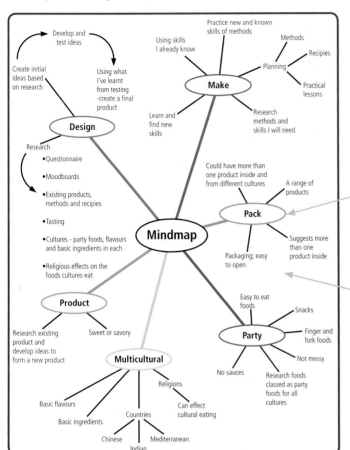

Make
- Using skills I already know
- Practice new and known skills of methods
- Planning
  - Methods
  - Recipies
  - Practical lessons
- Learn and find new skills
- Research methods and skills I will need

Design
- Develop and test ideas
- Create initial ideas based on research
- Using what I've learnt from testing -create a final product
- Research
  - Questionnaire
  - Moodboards
  - Existing products, methods and recipies
  - Tasting
  - Cultures - party foods, flavours and basic ingredients in each
  - Religious effects on the foods cultures eat

Mindmap

Pack
- Could have more than one product inside and from different cultures
- A range of products
- Suggests more than one product inside
- Packaging; easy to open

Product
- Research existing product and develop ideas to form a new product
- Sweet or savory

Multicultural
- Basic flavours
- Basic ingredients
- Religions
- Countries
  - Chinese
  - Indian
  - Mediterranean
- Can effect cultural eating

Party
- Easy to eat foods
- Snacks
- Finger and fork foods
- Not messy
- No sauces
- Research foods classed as party foods for all cultures

> Analysing the word 'Pack' shows the range of possibilities – should there be more than one product? Are there any restrictions, i.e. should it be easy to open? This area could be expanded so there are more details on the actual packaging – what materials will be used?

> Both students have worked out all the different kinds of research that needs to be carried out to help with design decisions. They have both also worked out that they need to use existing and new skills when making products, and need to experiment with ingredients and products.

> This student has explained what he needs to think about. For more marks the student could expand upon some of the ideas he has come up with. For example, what is the gender, age and health needs of the target group? What themes should he consider for the cake (birthday, Christmas, wedding)?

Example 2: C-grade project

C A K E S

DESIGN BRIEF

Design and make a celebration cake to be sold in a super-market retail store.

In order to be able to produce a celebration cake I will have think about lots of factors which will need to be considered. The spider diagram below shows some of the things I will be thinking about.

Analysis

Cakes for a super market.
- Storage – shelf life – packaging will it crush
- Nutritional value.
- Shape - Square Circle Triangle Other.
- Colour - Bright dull.
- Sweet.
- Size.
- Target group – who? – why?

Before I can begin to come up with some ideas for my cake I will need to carry out some research to to find out about the following:
- The type of cakes on sale - sweet colour.
- The normal shapes and size of cakes.
- The ranges of shapes in which cakes are made and sold, and if there popular to buy.
- People's preferences.
- Different textures of cakes.
- Types of fillings, flavourings and coatings used.
- Nutritional profile.
- Commonly used ingredients.
- Types of packaging used and how it protects the product.
- The recipe and methods used.

I will probably need to make different cake mixtures to see if they are able to be changed.

C A K E S

In this part of your coursework you must:

A GRADE Use a wide variety of appropriate sources to gather and order relevant research information.

C GRADE Use a variety of appropriate sources to gather and order relevant research information.

There is no point in completing research unless it is relevant. It is easy to spend a lot of time carrying out research only to find that it is of no use in helping you with design decisions. Looking at and tasting vegetarian meals will not help if your project outline is about healthy cakes. Looking at a video about how biscuits are made and the function of ingredients used will not be useful if your project outline is about barbecue products.

Research

Your research should help you to find out information that will make it easier to design the food products required by the project outline. It should help you to start designing ideas. This research can help you to find out:

★ what kind of products people like
★ what makes existing products good or bad
★ about the ingredients used in these kind of products
★ any restrictions or constraints you need to consider.

Your analysis of the project outline should have identified the kind of research activities you need to carry out. Section 1 in this book explains how to carry out this research.

Not all research has to be carried out at the beginning of your coursework. You can undertake research at any time during your coursework. For example, you could keep the packaging of one or two existing products you have sensory analysed. Towards the end of your coursework, when you have decided on your final product, you could use them as part of your research on packaging. A questionnaire might be more relevant after you have experimented with ingredients or modelled some prototypes, as you will have more idea about the kind of products you will make and the range of ingredients you will use.

Before you start any piece of research, it might be useful to write down what you hope to find out by completing the research and how you will use the information.

Presentation of research

Research work should be no more than two or three A3 pages (or six A4 pages) and only the results of your research are required. You should not spend hours writing up detailed information you have found out from your research; you need to spend most of your time making.

Think about the best way of presenting the information you have found out.

★ Questionnaire results can be presented in graph form, even if they are small.
★ Attribute profiles can also be reproduced at a small size.
★ Summarise what you have found out; do not copy pages of notes from books or the Internet. Identify the important facts and write about them in your own words.
★ More than one piece of research can be shown on a single page.

Make sure you read through your research. Does it 'tell a story' about what you have found out? Have you missed out some important things you have discovered?

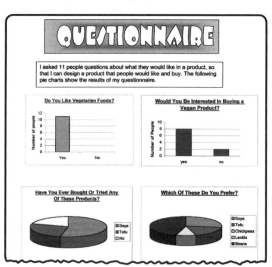

Use a computer where possible to present your findings

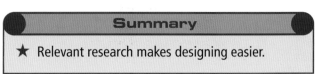

Summary

★ Relevant research makes designing easier.

Example 1: A-grade project

Heather Riddick

EXISTING PRODUCT TASTING CONT.

- **Indian Style Vegetable Feast- £1.98 from ASDA**

Includes; 4 Mini Vegetable Samosas, 6 Mini Onion Bhajis, 4 Aloo Tikkas and a wickedly hot chilli dip.

Described as being; 'Made with real Indian spices. For big nights in!'

The Packaging; The product has a fold over label, which shows the product being served onto a table, it makes it look good and quality. The product is contained in a black plastic tray with a clear film lid, which is to keep the price cheap.

The Product;
      Mini Vegetable Samosas- They look appetising and crispy, but slightly dry. There isn't much flavour and they aren't spicey enough. The texture of the filling is quite chewy and it doesn't have much of an after taste.
      It is much better with the dip, it brings out the flavours, it makes them much more spicy and better to eat.

Indian Style Vegetable feast-Mini Vegetable Samosas With Dip.

> *This tasting activity is detailed and has helped the student to know more about flavours and textures in relevant foods.*

Example 2: C-grade project

I looked in a number of different Food Technology books and found a lot of information on cook-chill products. For example:
*C.C.P has a long shelf life   *It is stored at 0-3 0c   *It can be cooked in a bulk
*It's used in such places as: Hospitals, Schools, Aircraft and trains, Factories
*It can be: Re-heated and served, Transported in chilled state and heated when served
*It needs to be heated at 72oC   *They are quite expensive   *They are ready meals
*They can either be "ready meals" or "Desserts"   * The food needs to be chilled as soon as possible * The meal needs to be heated properly and eaten with in 2 hours of being heated.

Videos

I have watched 2 videos about cooked chill products. One of these videos was called "Noon Products" and the other was "M&S meat marketing board". The first video showed people making Chicken korma and the second video showed how they made Cumberland Pie. I was surprised at how efficient and how many machines thare were. I learnt that they go through lots of different processes to get the quality standards that they need. M&S have complete control over the ingredients that go into the product. They even provide the farmer with seeds to grow the potatoes and they can trass back to were any of the ingredients come from. When they weigh there ingredients they are very accurate and do it a number of times. When a new product is made a number of people would taste it to make sure it is at the right standards.

> *This example has a summary of three different pieces of research – looking in textbooks to learn more about the cook chill process, watching videos to understand how products are mass produced and looking at existing products in supermarkets (this could be carried out on the Internet too). This student has successfully summarised what they have learnt, but they have not explained how they will use this information.*

Waitrose: In Waitrose I found out that there was a wider range of cook chill product meals than there was desserts. Most of the meals ranged between the price of £1.50-£3.50. Most of the products weighed between 300-400g. Hardly any of the products had special claims and most of the packages were quite boring and dull. All of the products were to be stored in a refrigerator and cooked in the microwave. The temperature in the chill cabinets were –1oC and had 2 days shelf life. The size portions of the products ranged between 1, 2 and 4, 1 being enough for 1 person. The was only 4 vegetarian products to choose from.

Sainsburys: There were hardly any cook chill desserts in sainsburys. Most of the prices of the meals ranged between £1.50-£3.00. The weights were between 400-700g. There were lots of special claims including "improved recipe" and "less then 5% fat". All of the meals were to be stored in the refrigerator and cooked in the microwave. Again the packaging was dull. The meals all had 1 day shelf life on them and the portion sizes of the meals were 1 or 2, 1 being enough for 1 person. There were hardly any vegetarian meals to choose from.

Supermarkets

M&S. There were quite a lot of desserts to choose from. The prices were between £1.00-£5.00. The weights ranged between 100-500g. The were quite a lot of special claims including

Asda: In Asda there were more cooked chill products meals to choose fro then desserts. The prices of the products ranged between £1.50-£3.00. The weights of the meals were all between 300-600g. In Asda there

7.3 Analysing research and generating ideas

In this part of your coursework you must:

A GRADE
1 Analyse the task and the research material logically, thoroughly and effectively.
2 Produce a detailed specification that focuses closely on the analysis.

C GRADE
1 Analyse the task and the research material.
2 Produce a specification that reflects the analysis.

Analysing research

You can analyse your research as you complete each type of research or you can analyse it all together as shown in the examples opposite.

The writing frame below might help you to put your thoughts down on paper. Your teacher can provide you with writing frames, such as this one, to present your coursework, but to gain the highest marks you must present your coursework in your own way. You must also look at the research sheet you produced while you were analysing the product to remind yourself about the information you gained from it.

When I completed my _____
research, I found out:

• _____

(add as many bullet points as you need)

I also found out _____

(do not just write down one point for each piece of research: aim for at least three things you have found out)

When I am designing, I will _____

(example: make sure my products are colourful)

This will help me when I design because

_____

(example: I will know to design products that contain cheese or chicken)

Outline specification

An outline specification is a list of properties a group of products must have and what the products should be like.

Your specification should reflect what the needs of the customer and producer are. For example, if your questionnaire shows that people prefer chicken rather than beef, your specification should say that most of your dishes will have chicken in them.

Activity

Before you write your outline specification, look again at pages 40 and 41.

Generating ideas

In this part of your coursework you must:

A GRADE Produce a wide range of distinct proposals that satisfy the specification.

C GRADE Produce a range of proposals that satisfy the specification.

Activity

Before you start to generate ideas, look again at Section 3 as the chapters here explain how to do this.

You should spend most of your time making, but you may want to complete further research to help you to come up with different product ideas. Look in recipe books or look for recipes on the Internet to create a mood board.

You need to write a list of proposed products that meet your outline specification, to which you could add some labelled sketches of initial ideas. You could then filter your ideas by deciding which ones are best. These will be your final ideas that you are going to trial and test by making them.

Only some ideas need to be made; you will not have time to make them all. You should choose to make the ideas that have good opportunities for development – those that will work best.

Write comments about all your ideas. Why have you chosen them? How do they match the outline specification? Do they match all the points of your specification or only a few? In this part, make sure you 'tell the story' and explain why you have selected these ideas. Alternatively, you could use a tick-box table to show how some ideas match the outline specification and some do not.

Working out what your ideas are is only a part of the ideas section of your coursework. Making these ideas is the most important part. There are different ways of doing this.

★ Try out lots of dishes. For example, for different vegetarian dishes, you could try vegetable curry, vegetable lasagne and Quorn shepherd's pie.

★ Model one particular idea in different ways using prototypes. For example, you could make a cheese and tomato bread where the ingredients are added in different ways such as in the whole mixture, in a layer or only on the top.

★ Experiment with one particular part of an idea. For example, work out what type of pastry you could use for a fruit flan or try different ways of colouring pasta for appearance and taste. Once you have chosen the best kind, make the whole product.

Do not forget that 60% of your coursework marks are for making skills. To gain good marks you need to demonstrate a wide range of skills during these making tasks.

Summary

★ Analysing makes you realise what you have found out and how you can use it.

★ Writing a specification makes you work out what you want your products to be like.

★ Trying lots of ideas gives you a good choice of dishes to develop.

Example 1: A-grade project

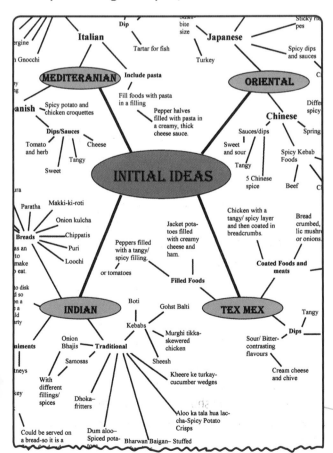

Example 2: C-grade project

Initial Ideas

- Butter bean bake
- Carrot Cheese bake
- Pasta salad
- Stuffed tomatoes & peppers
- Potato cheese & onion pie
- Potato cheese & parsley
- Vegetable cannelloni
- Stuffed peppers with rice & cheese
- Vegetarian Sausages
- Vegetable stir-fry
- Vegetable Burgers
- Spaghetti bolognaise
- Shepard's Pie (veggie)
- Quorn steaks & roast vegetable
- Vegetarian –kebabs
- Pizza
- Vegetable curry
- Jacket potatoes

This student has produced a range of proposals that satisfy the specification of a main course vegetarian meal. They then chose six of these ideas to try out, explaining why they chose them. Sketches and reasons for choosing and rejecting these ideas could add marks.

The initial ideas show a wide range of products from a variety of cultures. This student has spent time trying to find a wide range of proposals to satisfy the specification.

7.4 Planning and making

Planning

In this part of your coursework you must:

A GRADE Produce a correct sequence of activities that show where, why and how practical production decisions were made.

C GRADE Plan a largely correct and workable sequence of main making activities.

Time is an important consideration for food manufacturers and for you, not only during the design process but also when making products.

You can use charts to help you plan your time. You could use a Gantt chart to sequence all the tasks you must carry out during the design process. You could also use one to manage how long each task will take during production.

You could also use a flow chart to show how your final product can be made:
- as a one-off (in the classroom)
- as a mass-produced product, using large-scale equipment and quality controls.

You could also use an actual drawing of the production line for your final product. The examples of student work show some of the different ways to plan your activities.

Remember that you do not have to produce a production plan for every single product you have made or for every making task you have carried out. You need to produce a plan for your final product.

Making

In this part of your coursework you must:
A GRADE
1 Record and justify the need for any changes or adaptations.
2 Use appropriate materials, components, equipment and processes (including CAM) consistently, correctly, skilfully and safely.
3 Make a complete product of high quality.

4 Demonstrate an ability to satisfy accurately and completely all the demands of the design solution.
5 Thoroughly consider quality assurance and quality controls and apply them consistently and successfully.
C GRADE
1 Recognise the need for and justify any changes or adaptations.
2 Use appropriate materials, components, equipment and processes (including CAM) consistently, correctly, skilfully and safely.
3 Produce a complete, effective and well-assembled outcome.
4 Demonstrate a level of accuracy and finish in the product that satisfies most of the demands of the design solution.
5 Clearly use quality assurance and quality control in most activities.

Making is the most important part of your coursework; it is the area where you can gain about 40% of your GCSE mark. If you do not make enough, you will not give yourself the chance to gain the best marks you can in this section.

Making is not just making a complete product. Making is:
★ experimenting with ingredients
★ modelling parts of a product or making small quantities of a product (prototypes)
★ tasting existing products
★ nutritional analysis of ingredients and recipes
★ comparison testing of shop-bought and homemade products
★ batch production of a food product
★ making one-off products.

You can see that there are lots of opportunities for you to demonstrate your skills.

When you come to write evaluations of all your making tasks, you will be able to show any changes or adaptations you would make. If you carry out a range of making tasks, you will be able to show that:
★ you can use the right ingredients for the task
★ you have an understanding of the processes involved in making products – you understand the method

★ you can use appropriate equipment for the task. This includes CAM such as bread machines, ice cream machines, digital scales and electronic mixers. It also includes simple equipment, such as biscuit cutters and rolling guides, that will help you achieve the same quality product every time you make the product.

★ you have carried out quality control procedures during making activities because you have produced a complete product of high quality. These controls include health and safety controls such as appropriate storage of ingredients.

Therefore, making is not separate to designing; they have links with each other. There should be evidence of quality control and quality assurance as you make and in your design folder.

Summary

★ Making activities should be seen as the most important part of your coursework.

> This is an easy-to-read production plan for a one-off product to be made in the classroom. More detail could be included on the size of some of the ingredients used. Sequencing could also be shown by moving the rice flow chart next to the curry flow chart.

Example 1: A-grade project

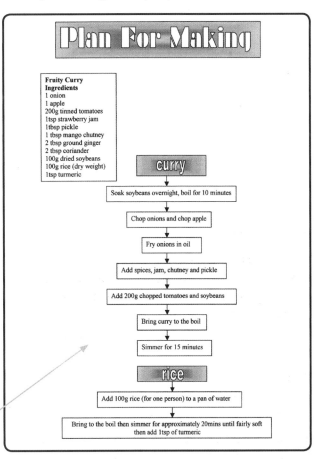

Plan For Making

Fruity Curry Ingredients
1 onion
1 apple
200g tinned tomatoes
1tsp strawberry jam
1tbsp pickle
1 tbsp mango chutney
2 tbsp ground ginger
2 tbsp coriander
100g dried soybeans
100g rice (dry weight)
1tsp turmeric

curry

Soak soybeans overnight, boil for 10 minutes

Chop onions and chop apple

Fry onions in oil

Add spices, jam, chutney and pickle

Add 200g chopped tomatoes and soybeans

Bring curry to the boil

Simmer for 15 minutes

rice

Add 100g rice (for one person) to a pan of water

Bring to the boil then simmer for approximately 20mins until fairly soft then add 1tsp of turmeric

Example 2: C-grade project

> This is a good example of a plan that shows the mass production of a product in a visual way.

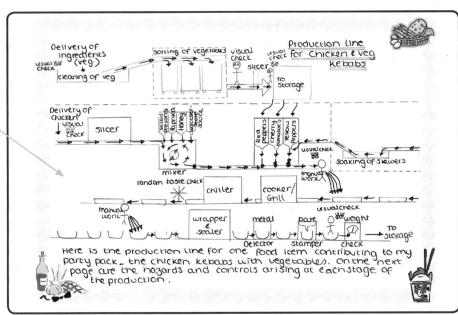

Evaluating and communicating

In this part of your coursework you must:

A GRADE

1 **Test, objectively evaluate and effectively modify your work throughout the process as appropriate.**

2 **Select and skilfully use a wide range of communication, graphical and ICT skills, which have helped to clarify your thinking and are sufficient to convey ideas to yourself and others effectively and precisely.**

C GRADE

1 **Test, evaluate and modify your work throughout the process as appropriate.**

2 **Use a range of communication, graphical and ICT skills sufficient to convey ideas to yourself and others.**

Evaluating

It is important to learn how to evaluate and to present coursework in an easy-to-read way. This often means using ICT skills.

 **Activity**

Before you evaluate in your coursework, look again at pages 52 and 53 to see how to evaluate a practical making activity.

The examples of evaluations shown here are evaluations for a single whole product that has been made. If you are experimenting with particular ingredients or modelling using prototypes, your evaluation needs to be planned in a different way. Your evaluation might include less detail on the process and more on the results you got from the different tests you carried out on the products such as comparison, ranking and rating tests.

How to evaluate

1 Write several bullet points for each item.

2 Explain why you have made the product (if you have not already said so).

3 Comment on how your practical went. What did you find difficult? What did you find easy? Did one particular task take longer than you thought? You may want to comment here on how easy it would be to mass produce your product. You will use this information to help you if you develop the product and make it again.

4 Comment in detail on the tests you carried out to find out how your dish turned out. What did it taste like? How did it look? What was its smell and texture like? Include other people's comments (at least two others) as well as your own thoughts. Completing an attribute profile is not enough; you must write descriptive sentences, too.

5 Explain how the product does or does not match your outline or product specification. Use the word 'because' a lot in this paragraph. For example, 'This chicken curry matches my product specification because it is…'

6 Explain how you could improve, modify or adapt the product if you made it again. This should match up with the comments made about the product.

Communicating

The content of your coursework is the most important thing. It has to be detailed and to 'tell a story' of your design process. However, you also need to think about how you present your work – how you communicate your thoughts and ideas to others.

Do not:
★ spend a long time designing titles for each page or adding pretty borders: these will not get you extra marks.

Do:
★ use skills you have learnt in other subjects such as ICT skills
★ use the skills you have developed during your GCSE course such as nutritional analysis
★ present your work neatly and precisely in the most visually interesting way possible.

The examples here show some of the following uses of ICT:
★ word-processing – this does not get any ICT marks, but it may make your work clearer
★ spreadsheets to create graphs and present sensory evaluation results. They can also be used to present

information from questionnaires and for costing exercises
★ nutritional analysis programs to analyse ingredients
★ digital images of the product made. You could also use pictures of packaging, a step in the process, special ingredients and special activities such as a tasting panel
★ drawing programs, such as Coral Draw, could be used to design a packaging net. Coral Draw includes ready-made bar codes that can be used.

Summary

★ Evaluating practical activities in detail will help with further design decisions.

★ Good communication skills will also aid decisions.

Example 1: A-grade project

EVALUATION

Evaluation of My Lentil Balls with Sweet and Sour Sauce

To make the lentil balls I boiled the lentils then mixed them with mash potato to bind the mixture when shaped into balls, which I fried. I also made the sauce by chopping vegetables and frying them in oil, vinegar and water.

The lentil balls were soft in the middle but didn't stay together very well. They were slightly crunchy around the outside but not very. The sweet and sour sauce was colourful and aromatic and it tasted both sweet and tart and had a good flavour and saucy texture

My mum and I both thought that the sweet and sour sauce tasted really nice and was full of flavour but there needed to be more of the sauce. I didn't think the lentil balls had enough flavour and I didn't think they were crispy enough around the outside, but my dad thought they had a good firm outer coating and squidgy middle, which he liked.

To improve my dish I would add more water to the sauce to make more of it and I would chop the vegetables a bit finer because the sauce was a little too chunky and so it didn't cover the lentil balls very well. I would also add some flavouring to the lentil balls possibly coriander or paprika to make them a bit spicy. I might also add some tomato puree to give them a more "tomatoey" flavour and add some vegetables like pepper, carrot, peas or sweet corn. I could also coat them in flour and water to help bind them and fry them in a deep fat fryer, which might seal them better than frying them in a pan.

Attribute Profile of my Sweet and Sour Lentil Balls

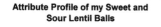

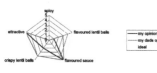

Nutrition Information - lentil balls + rice		
	Typical values	
	per 100 g	per serving 220 g
Energy	762 kJ	1676 kJ
	182 kcal	401 kcal
Protein	7.74 g	17 g
Carbohydrate	37.4 g	82.4 g
of which Sugar	3.84 g	8.44 g
Fat	1.22 g	2.69 g
of which Saturates	0.27 g	0.59 g
Fibre (NSP)	1.9 g	4.19 g
Sodium	0.02 g	0.05 g
Iron	2.1 mg	4.62 mg
Calcium	32.1 mg	70.7 mg
Vitamin A	17.7 ug	38.8 ug
Thiamine (B1)	0.26 mg	0.58 mg
Riboflavin (B2)	0.06 mg	0.13 mg
Niacin	1.76 mg	3.86 mg
Vitamin C	18.2 mg	40.1 mg
Vitamin D	0 ug	0 ug

This is a picture of my sweet and sour lentil balls.

I think it fitted my specification because:
• It was colourful and attractive
• It was cultural because it was Chinese
• There was protein in the lentils
• It contained lots of vegetables and some fruit
• It was tasty and filling
It didn't fit my specification because:
• The lentil balls didn't have enough flavour

Example 2: C-grade project

Evaluation of idea 1

I thought that my practical went very well, it was quite easy to make, I didn't not find anything really hard excepted trying to cut the Mozzarella cheese up because it was like trying to cut up rubber. I think it would be easy to make large quantities because you would just double everything.

My lasagne was very nice and I was pleased with it, all the layers went together very well. I thought that it could of done with some more tomatoes, tomato puree and a little bit more of garlic. It had a good texture to it; the top layer was nice and crispy round the outside of the edges with the cheese melted on the top. I put cottage cheese in some of the layers so it went together well. My mum and dad had the lasagne as well for their tea and they thought it needed more tomatoes, tomato puree and garlic in it. They said that it was a good size family meal. But they were surprised how nice the quorn was and they would use it again as a meat subsitute.

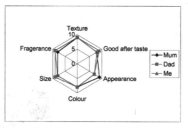

My lasagne dish did match my General specification a bit e.g. suitable for vegetarians, filling, cook chill and have a flavour in it.

I could improve my lasagne dish by adding some vegetables in it, adding more tomatoes, tomato puree and more garlic in it and make a cheese sauce instead of just putting pieces of cheese on it.

The first section lacks detail about the processes used to make the lasagne. Good descriptive words are used to show the testing carried out. Some comments are too subjective rather than objective. Matching to the specification is far too brief and lacks explanation. Modifications are suggested but they do not all follow on from previous comments.

A comment about what the student did for the lentil balls practical has been added, but more marks could have been awarded if the student had commented on what they found easy or difficult. The student has completed a nutritional analysis of the product but then not commented on this further. There were good comments on the taste of the product and these were followed through with detailed suggestions on how to improve the product. The way the student analysed its match to the specification was good.

Development 1: Product specification

In this part of your coursework you must:

A GRADE

1 Use one or more of your proposals and relevant knowledge of techniques, manufacturing and working characteristics to develop a detailed and coherent design solution.

2 (Produce a detailed specification that focuses closely on the analysis.)

C GRADE

1 Use your proposals and relevant knowledge to develop a detailed design solution that satisfies the specification.

2 (Produce a specification that reflects the analysis.)

This part of your coursework is the most important section. Developing a solution that matches your specification shows your overall understanding of the design process. How you develop dishes will depend on how you tested and trialled your ideas.

Activity

Before you develop your coursework ideas, look again at pages 50 and 51.

Developing trialled ideas

If you have tried several whole dishes from your ideas, you now need to work out which one you could develop for your final product. Then you need to consider how you can develop the product to make it better.

Example 1 shows a student who trialled eight initial ideas for a vegan main course product. They have made complete products first. The student has used a table to analyse the work by evaluating the ideas against the outline specification. This table is a good visual aid that makes it easy to identify the success of each product against the specification.

The student decided to develop two ideas at this stage and has shown how they think one of these (ravioli) can be modified to improve it. They went on to complete a lot of making: developing the pasta during one lesson, the filling

for the ravioli during another and the sauce during a final lesson. The student worked on developing different parts of the product.

Experimenting with initial ideas

If you have experimented with the ingredients and/or components of some of your ideas, you have already completed some development work. You may have decided that you did not like the outcome of this experimentation and that you want to experiment with another product – this is fine. There is no right way to carry out your coursework. If you evaluate all practical work carried out and justify each step you take, you are following the design process. Just remember that you must produce a wide range of distinct ideas that you must develop in detail.

Product specification

A product specification is a list of properties that a single product must have. It is a list of what it should be like.

Activity

Before you write the product specification in your coursework, look again at pages 52 and 53.

Completing the table in example 1 made the task of writing a product specification easier. The specifications are for one product each. The outline specification that you wrote after completing research was for several products. A product specification can be more precise and detailed on several points, especially on the taste, texture, appearance, nutrition and size of the product.

Writing a product specification is important during the final parts of the design process. If you evaluate the product against a detailed product specification, instead of an outline specification, you will produce a high-quality product that really does match all the points of the specification. Example 2 has detailed comments about the appearance, taste, texture, nutrition and size of the product. This is a good checklist to use when evaluating.

You should include the following in a product specification:
★ the target group the product is aimed at

★ what it should look like
★ what kind of taste it should have
★ the kind of texture or textures it should have
★ the size/weight and dimensions of the product
★ how long its shelf life will be and where it will be stored
★ its nutritional content such as high in fibre
★ the type of packaging it will have
★ the general quantities it will be made in such as batch produced
★ the selling price.

Once you have developed your ideas and are satisfied that the product now matches the product specification, you will be able to write a detailed manufacturing specification that explains how the product should be made every time. This means the product can be mass or batch produced.

Example 1: A-grade project

Analysis of Ideas

Points of specification→ dishes↓	Suitable for vegetarians	Suitable for vegans	colourful	tasty	filling	Contains protein	cultural	Suitable for mass production
Lasagne	√ 10	√ 10	√ 8	√ 9	√ 10	√ 10	√ 10	√ 7
Shepherds pie	√ 10	√ 10	√ 7	√ 9	√ 9	√ 10	X 3	√ 7
Spaghetti and bean balls	√ 10	√ 10	√ 9	√ 8	√ 9	√ 9	X 3	√ 7
Paella	√ 10	√ 10	X 4	√ 9	√ 10	√ 9	√ 10	√ 10
Sweet and sour lentil balls	√ 10	√ 10	√ 10	√ 9	√ 9	√ 9	√ 10	√ 7
Lentil curry	√ 10	√ 10	√ 7	√ 9	√ 9	√ 9	√ 10	√ 10
Ravioli	√ 10	X 0	X 2	X 3	√ 10	√ 10	√ 10	√ 6
Tikka masala	√ 10	√ 10	√ 7	X 1	X 3	√ 10	√ 10	√ 10

A lot of my dishes scored very highly when their suitability was matched against points of my specification. I have chosen to develop the ravioli and tikka masala because I found these were the least satisfying of my ideas.

I have done a table which compares my ideas to points on my specification. I have either ticked or crossed them depending on whether I felt the idea fulfilled its criteria and also given it a score out of 10 to show how well I felt it met each point of my specification, because, for example, lots of my ideas were colourful, but some were more colourful than others.

How I will develop them:
Ravioli
    I will have to use a filling that does not contain cheese or any other animal product so that it will be suitable for vegans.
I will try these fillings:
  • Sun dried tomato.
  • Vegan substitute cheese slices.
To improve the colour I could do the following things:
  • Use spinach to colour the pasta.
  • Use tomato puree to colour the pasta.
  • Use a colouring spice such as turmeric or saffron (although this might not work well with pasta.)
  • Make an alternative sauce:
To change the sauce I will:
  • Make a tomato sauce.
  • Add coloured peppers to the sauce.

Summary

★ Developing products is the most important part of your coursework.

★ Detailed product specifications help you to evaluate how successful your developments are.

Example 2: A-grade project

PRODUCT SPECIFICATION

Ravioli
  • It will be a vegan main course meal.
  • It will have soft pasta dough.
  • The pasta and sauce will both have an appropriate and attractive colour.
  • Each piece of ravioli will be in a semi circle shape with a diameter of 7cm (folded over).
  • It will have a tasty filling.
  • It will be a nutritious and healthy meal.
  • It will contain 35% protein, 50% carbohydrate and 15% fat.
  • It will be low in sugar and fat and high in fibre.
  • It will have a tasty sauce.
  • It will appeal to people interested in vegan, vegetarian and Italian food.

Curry
  • It will be a vegan main course meal.
  • It will be an attractive colour.
  • It will be pleasantly aromatic.
  • It will be full of flavour.
  • It will contain protein.
  • It will be a nutritious and healthy meal.
  • It will contain 35% protein, 50% carbohydrate and 15% fat.
  • It will be low in sugar, low in fat and high in fibre.
  • It will have a spicy curry sauce.
  • It will be suitable to be sold in a pack with 200g curry and 100g rice.
  • It will be suitable for mass production.
  • It will appeal to people interested in vegan, vegetarian and Indian food.

This product specification is fairly detailed. A little more description could be used to explain the exact taste required, rather than just 'tasty', and the exact colour could also have been described.

This sheet clearly shows that the student has analysed their ideas, but a total tally of the results would have been helpful. It also looks at why the student has chosen the two dishes to prototype before going on to explain how one of them might be developed.

7.7 Development 2: Improving your product and packaging

In this part of your coursework you must:

A GRADE Use one or more of your proposals and relevant knowledge of techniques, manufacturing and working characteristics to develop a detailed and coherent design solution.

C GRADE Use your proposals and relevant knowledge to develop a detailed design solution that satisfies the specification.

Improving and developing your product

Developing is:
★ modelling prototypes (using small quantities of ingredients to make more than one outcome)
★ experimenting with ingredients.

Developing is not, for example:
★ adding more seasoning to your product because you forgot to add salt and pepper
★ piping the mashed potato onto a shepherd's pie instead of using a fork to make it look nice

However, developing the seasoning of a dish can be a part of development. For example, make a dish such as a basic meat sauce made with onions, minced beef, flour and water. Divide the mixture equally into a number of bowls. Add different varieties and/or quantities of seasoning, such as herbs and spices, measuring the quantities of seasoning carefully into each bowl. Use comparison tests with at least three people to decide which sauce has the best flavour.

Developing the appearance of a dish is a development but several ways need to be tried at the same time. Using the example of a shepherd's pie, make a quantity of mashed potato. Spread small amounts onto three ovenproof dishes. Sprinkle grated cheese on one and breadcrumbs on another. Leave the third one plain. Pipe potato onto a fourth dish. Cook all four dishes and use comparison tests to see which is preferred.

Both of the above developments can be done in a single lesson if they are planned carefully. These two making tasks

would mean that the product has been developed in detail to reach a detailed design solution. This is because the results of development work have helped to refine the final product.

Planning

Good development work only happens if you plan your practicals well. Good development work is when more than one experiment or modification is carried out at one time. You have to plan carefully for these kinds of lessons as they often mean you need to have lots of small amounts of ingredients. You could consider working with a partner who is completing the same or similar project. When you plan your practical, you must consider how easy it will be to get the ingredients and how costly it could be.

Packaging

Nearly all food products sold to consumers are packaged. It is important that you understand about different types of packaging used for food products.

If you have saved some packaging from your research of existing products, you could evaluate these, especially features such as how the essential information is conveyed to the customer. You then need to use this knowledge to work out the best packaging for your final product.

There are two parts of packaging you need to comment on:
★ the materials used for both inner and outer packaging, and comment on environmental issues
★ the information included on the package.

Remember that the design elements, such as use of colour, pictures, fonts and descriptive words, need only a brief comment or no comment at all.

Although packaging is part of developing a solution, it is a small part. You should spend most of your time on making tasks. Remember, too, that you do not have to make the packaging; you just need to show that you have considered it.

Example 1: A-grade project

This pasta development is quite simple. Small quantities of different pasta have been made, cooked and tested so that the best can be used for ravioli. This is an example of developing a component part of a product by modelling with prototypes. This sheet is also a good example of effective presentation: use of boxes to divide text and graphs to present results in a visual way.

Development

Because I am trying to develop my pasta dish I am going to try making different types of pasta and comparing them. I will make pasta with soya flour pasta with semolina flour and flour and also pasta with semolina flour, flour and egg, as a control.

Pasta Ingredients	Evaluation
50g Soya flour water	There wasn't much to the ingredients of this pasta and it became a very brown looking dough which was fairly unattractive! When it was boiled it tasted hard, dense and had an unusual nutty and not altogether pleasing taste.

Pasta Ingredients	Evaluation
50g Semolina 150g Flour water	This pasta came out soggy, it came apart a lot and although it still had its "pasta taste", the structure and texture made it gooey and unpleasant.

Pasta Ingredients	Evaluation
50g Semolina 150g Flour water 1 egg	This pasta came out smooth; it was strong and held its shape. It had the best taste and texture out of all the pastas tested on this page.

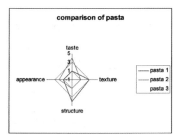

comparison of pasta

Overall from this development investigation I have found that the best pasta to make is pasta with egg. Unfortunately this is no good for my ravioli because vegans do not eat egg. Therefore it would not fit my specification.

This development of a dip includes several developments all carried out in one practical task. Before the practical, the student decided to add cottage cheese for added texture. They also used a nutritional analysis program to work out its nutritional content and then worked out how to reduce the fat content. This is a well planned and imaginative development.

Example 2: A-grade project

Evaluation of Developments

Dip

The dip started off with just mayonnaise, minced garlic and chopped chives but I wanted to add a better texture so I added cottage cheese. I knew that this gave a crunchier texture therefore I decided to continue with this recipe and build it by adding more ingredients.

On my way, I nutritionally analysed the dip and found hat it was quite high in fat— 17 g per 100 g. This told me I needed to reduce the fat content. I did this by using low fat mayonnaise and low fat cottage cheese instead of the 'normal' ones. The flavour wasn't altered and nutrition had increased.

The specification required me to add a herb to he dip. I needed to find out what herb so I made the dip as normal and made some plain breadsticks to taste it with. I divided the dip into four equal pots and laid them out on a work top. In each pot except one, which I left plain, I added a different herb and numbered each pot so that the names gave no biased opinions to the dips. I then let three friends taste each dip in turn sipping water in between tasting each dip. The herbs which I used were oregano, marjoram and thyme. I found that the oregano was slightly stronger than the marjoram whilst the thyme gave a totally different flavour which didn't blend well with the garlic taste. My friends all agreed with my opinion as you can see from the star diagram. They all preferred the marjoram dip. From this I decided to use this dip for my final dip.

Star Diagram Showing 3 Peoples' Preferred Vegetable

There was just one thing left that I needed to solve. Ten specification stated that I must use a bio-degradable container. I did some research into what sort of containers already existed. I found that most came in a plastic pot but in a recipe book I saw some stuffed peppers which inspired me to use a hollow pepper as the container. I decided to use a green pepper as I tried red, yellow, orange and green yet the green seemed to be the best as it matched the green pieces of herbs in the dip.

Summary

★ Developing ideas to meet the needs of the outline or product specification is the most important part of the design process.

★ Developing in the depth required for a good grade is all about planning.

★ You need to consider the materials of your packaging and the information to be included, but you do not have to make it.

Industrial practices

In this part of your coursework you must:

A GRADE Provide evidence that you have considered and taken account of relevant issues, industrial practices, and systems and control.

C GRADE Provide evidence of having considered relevant issues, industrial practices, and systems and control.

You must consider industrial practices and relevant points, such as environmental issues, throughout your coursework. You need to know what restrictions industrial practices will put on the products you are trialling. For example, is the product suitable for manufacturing in large quantities? Are the ingredients inexpensive?

If you are unclear about the restrictions large-scale production will impose, you do not know the cost of your ingredients or you do not know which kind of packaging is biodegradable, you must carry out research. Not all research has to be carried out at the beginning of the project; some research is best considered once the design solution is near the final stage so that the research can be relevant for that particular product. It can be carried out when it is appropriate.

Costing

Costing is easy to do using a spreadsheet and Internet supermarket websites to research the prices of ingredients. Costing can be carried out throughout your coursework, or it can be done at the idea stage. Costing can also be an important part of your development. For example, cheese is an expensive ingredient. Developing a low-price pizza for mass production means experimenting with the quantities of cheese used on the pizza so that the cost is as low as possible. The price of manufacture is an important industrial issue. Example 1 shows a costing sheet. The student has calculated the cost of making their product for four people and from this total have worked out the cost per portion.

Example 1: A-grade project

Costing

I have worked out the costing for my product, using the prices of my ingredients and the amounts I used in my recipe, which produced enough for 4 people. From this I worked out the cost to make a portion for one person, with the reduced cost of ingredients from bulk buying.

ingredients	Grams of food per ingredient	Weight of food per pack	Cost of food per pack	Actual cost of product
tinned tomatoes	200	400	£0.37	£0.19
granny smith apples	125	1000	£1.19	£0.15
onions	150	1000	£1.09	£0.16
turmeric	2	10	£0.36	£0.07
vegetable oil	14	1000	£1.04	£0.01
rice	400	100	£0.09	£0.36
jam	15	100	£0.14	£0.02
pickle	20	1000	£1.79	£0.04
chutney	20	100	£0.39	£0.08
ground ginger	2	10	£0.38	£0.08
coriander	2	10	£0.59	£0.12
soybeans	100	500	£0.99	£0.20
Total cost of ingredients for one off production				£1.47

Number of Portions: 4

Price per portion: £0.37

Cost after bulk buying: £0.28

Expected retail price: £0.92

Having looked at existing products of a similar nature such as Stella McCartney's Shepherds pie priced at £1.49, I think that £1.20 would be a suitable retail price. My meal would be quite cheap in comparison to other meals, but would still make a considerable amount of profit from sale. I chose a slightly higher price than the expected retail price on my costing, so that my meal wouldn't appear too cheap and put consumers off, by suggesting low quality.

I would mass produce my product in a pack suitable for one person because this is the size of meal that people indicated that they would prefer to purchase in my market research questionnaire. I also think that quick ready made meals would appeal more to a person who would otherwise have to cook for just themselves. But my product might also be suitable for producing in packs for 2 or 4 people as well.

Pie Chart to show breakdown of selling price

Products vary considerably, the percentages are provided ONLY to give a rough guide

This a good costing sheet where the student has worked out that their final product will be retailed for £1.20. They have remembered the research they carried out – on existing products, their size and retail price – at the beginning of their coursework.

Systems and control

Writing a HACCP plan like the one below will show that you recognise that health and safety is an important industrial issue. Once you start cooking on a larger scale than just you and your family, hygiene is a major consideration. You must produce a safe food product.

A systems flow chart could also be included to show feedback and controls. The use of CAM could also be identified in the system to ensure quality products are made.

Example 2: C-grade project

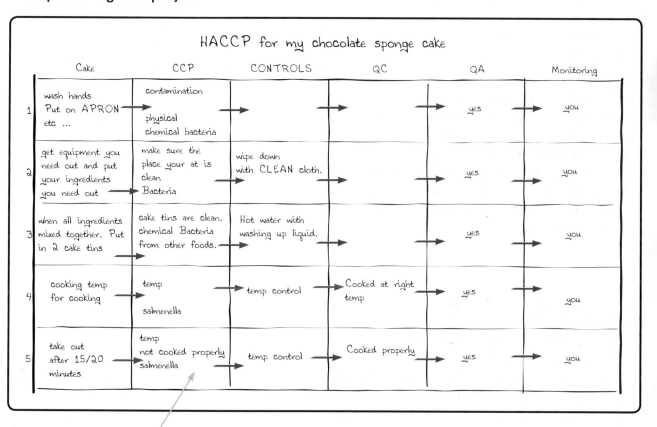

HACCP for my chocolate sponge cake

	Cake	CCP	CONTROLS	QC	QA	Monitoring
1	wash hands Put on APRON etc ...	contamination physical chemical bacteria			yes	you
2	get equipment you need out and put your ingredients you need out	make sure the place your at is clean Bacteria	wipe down with CLEAN cloth.		yes	you
3	when all ingredients mixed together. Put in 2 cake tins	cake tins are clean. chemical Bacteria from other foods.	Hot water with washing up liquid.		yes	you
4	cooking temp for cooking	temp salmenella	temp control	Cooked at right temp	yes	you
5	take out after 15/20 minutes	temp not cooked properly salmenella	temp control	Cooked properly	yes	you

This is a simple HACCP plan for a low risk food product. The page is set out well but the process does not include storage of ingredients and the final product. It also does not break down the actual process of making into separate steps. For example, weighing and mixing. Specific temperatures should also be mentioned, such as below 5°C and above 70°C for 2 minutes.

Manufacturing specification

A manufacturing or final product specification is a detailed specification written once the final product has been developed. It explains exactly what the product will be and how it will be made. It can be a mixture of statements, illustrations and flow charts. A manufacturing specification should provide enough information about the product to enable anyone to use the specification and make the same product again and again. The specification should contain:

★ product title
★ product description
★ product weight
★ storage conditions
★ shelf life
★ nutritional composition
★ ingredients as a percentage of total
★ country of origin
★ process information (how the product is made)
★ a copy of the HACCP data sheet – see page 85
★ critical control points
★ chemical and microbiological standards (the very small amounts of chemicals and bacteria that are allowed to be in the food)
★ sensory profile (attributes and description that show appearance, taste and texture required)
★ allergen information
★ suitability for vegetarians, vegans, coeliacs, kosher, halal, organic, GM-free
★ packaging information (description, materials including grade, dimensions).

Other processes that you carry out during your coursework also show industrial practices like those that food manufacturers carry out during their product development. These include:

★ using questionnaires
★ using sensory analysis
★ using spreadsheets to analyse data
★ carrying out nutritional analysis using CAD
★ scaling-up ingredients
★ identifying the function of ingredients
★ identifying equipment used.

Final evaluation

When you have completed your coursework and produced a good-quality final product, you must do one more thing: write a final evaluation. This is a summative evaluation instead of all the formative evaluations you have written during your coursework. It rounds off your coursework and 'finishes the story'. It explains how successful your final product is – if it matches the specifications.

Summary

★ Final products must be developed in an industrial context. This means they must be suitable for food manufacture.

Preparing for the exam

Forty per cent of your GCSE grade comes from the final exam you will take in the summer at the end of your course.

On 1 March of the year in which you will take the exam, you will be given a preparation sheet. This double-sided, A4 preparation sheet gives you the theme and context of some of the exam questions. Therefore, before the exam, you will know the kind of food products some of the questions will be on. First, there is written information giving you background information on the design project the exam will be based on. Second, there is further information about this context in colour and diagram form on the back of the sheet.

In the exam you will probably be asked:
★ about how to research and write specifications for the theme and context
★ to design and develop one or two products
★ about how these products are made and the function of their ingredients
★ how these products are made in industry.

You will have up to ten weeks to prepare for the exam. If you use this time well, you will have time to:
★ have practical experience of the food products mentioned on the preparation sheet
★ practise producing design ideas of these products
★ revise other topics mentioned on the preparation sheet.

As well as this, you will need to revise thoroughly all the topics you have covered over the two-year course.

What's in this section?

8.1 Disassembling the preparation sheet

In this chapter you will:

★ learn how to use the preparation sheet to guide you in your revision.

General Certificate of Secondary Education
June 2004
Foundation and Higher Examination

PREPARATION SHEET FOR THE 2004 EXAMINATION 3542/52PM

Design and Technology: Food Technology
(For the Foundation and Higher Tiers of the Full and Short Courses)

Instructions

• This Preparation Sheet will be given to you on or after 1 March 2004. The context for some of the examination questions is given below and further information is given overleaf.

• Between 1 March and the examination date you will have the opportunity to research the context with the guidance of your teacher.

• No Preparation Sheets or any associated material may be taken into the examination room.

RESEARCH CONTEXT: MULTI-CULTURAL
DESIGN THEME: READY PREPARED VEGETABLE PRODUCTS

In preparation for the examination you should:

1 research

   • the properties and functions of ingredients used in multi-cultural vegetable products;

   • the role of computers in the development and costing of new products.

2 consider how initial design ideas can be developed into final products.

3 investigate

   • how production methods and control systems are used to produce quality outcomes that are safe to eat;

   • the use of freezing as a method of extending the shelf-life of vegetable products;

   • the packaging and labelling of ready prepared vegetable products.

For Higher Tiers only
Candidates should also study the increasing popularity of organic vegetables.

TP/0204/3542/52PM   **3542/52PM**

Make sure you read through the preparation sheet carefully

You will need to read the front page of the preparation sheet very carefully. This should help you to work out what you already know and what you need to revise in more detail.

Step 1

You need to analyse the research context and design theme words. Think about what they mean. You probably did this with your design brief for your coursework, so you should have had practise at doing this before. Each word needs to be analysed carefully.

For example:

RESEARCH CONTEXT: MULTICULTURAL

'Multicultural' means foods from other countries or foods that will appeal to the tastes of more than one country.

DESIGN THEME: READY-PREPARED VEGETABLE PRODUCT

'Ready-prepared' could mean anything from microwave-ready meals to chopped salad leaves.

'Vegetable' refers to a plant or part of a plant that is used for food. There are hundreds of vegetables, ranging from leaves to dried beans.

'Product' could mean a whole meal, a snack or a side dish.

Step 2

Look at the information given in the section that begins, 'In preparation for the examination, you should…'. This will suggest some things to think about before the exam. Once you have read this section, you should think about all the work you completed for your coursework. This knowledge can be applied to this preparation work such as research techniques like looking at existing products and carrying out sensory analysis. Other information in this section will identify certain parts of the syllabus that you need to revisit and revise in detail.

For example:

'In preparation for the examination, you should investigate the use of freezing as a method of extending the shelf life of vegetable products.'

This suggests careful revision of freezing, as well as revising other methods of preservation, such as chilling and canning, so that comparisons could be made between the two different methods.

Step 3

The illustrated back page gives you clues on particular questions that will be asked and the kind of food products you should be researching. Here are two things you can do at this stage.

1 Extend the mind map as shown below.

2 Work out the kind of questions that could be asked about the items in the illustrations.

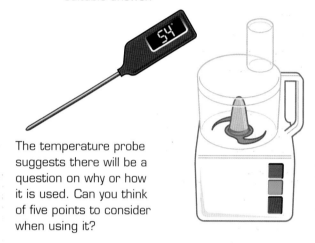

The food processor suggests there will be a question asking how electrical equipment helps in the production of quality outcomes. As part of your revision, you could plan a suitable answer.

The temperature probe suggests there will be a question on why or how it is used. Can you think of five points to consider when using it?

Other elements on the preparation sheet

On the preparation sheet there is usually something extra for students taking the higher-mark paper or for those taking the full course rather than the short course. Make sure you identify this part of the sheet and check with your teacher if you need to revise this area.

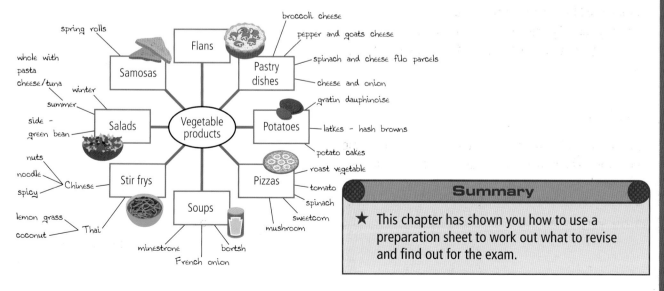

Summary
★ This chapter has shown you how to use a preparation sheet to work out what to revise and find out for the exam.

In this chapter you will:

★ learn how to carry out practical preparation for the exam.

On the preparation sheet, you will usually be asked to find out about the properties and functions of ingredients used in the food products identified there. It will be easier to understand these properties and functions if you have actually eaten, made and experimented with these products. As you have six to ten weeks to prepare for the exam, you should have time to complete practical sessions on the products mentioned in the design theme. These sessions follow the same pattern as the ones you carried out for your coursework.

Product evaluations

The first thing to do is to complete product evaluations on several products relevant to the theme and context of the exam. You should aim for at least three products, but preferably more. If you work in groups, this should not be expensive. You could even carry out more product evaluations at home. For example, for the research context and design theme 'Multicultural, ready-prepared vegetable products', you might evaluate as follows:

RESEARCH CONTEXT: MULTICULTURAL READY-PREPARED VEGETABLE PRODUCTS

1   a vegetable quiche
2   a mediterranean roast vegetable pizza
3   vegetable samosas or spring rolls
4   a vegetable curry or Indian vegetable side dish
5   a baked potato dish
6   a tinned vegetable and pasta soup

Look again at pages 8 and 9 to remind yourself how to carry out a product evaluation and about the wide range of information you can get from this activity. Make sure you look at the ingredients on the packaging and the nutritional information. Write down comments on appearance, taste and texture. Keep the packaging to analyse later.

This product evaluation can last more than one lesson. It is an essential part to the preparation of the exam as it gives you good experience of the food products that will be discussed in the exam.

Making products

You could spend time gaining practical experience of making some of the food products. For example, you could make at least three different products so that you are confident about the processes involved in creating them. Evaluate each product once you have made them in the same way as you evaluated the food products you made during your coursework. Comment on how easy each one was to make and how easy it would be to make it in large quantities. You could also comment on the product's sensory properties and on how it could be improved or modified if you made it again. Use these evaluations as part of your revision notes.

Function of ingredients

To help you find out the functions and properties of ingredients, when you have completed each practical you could write a list of ingredients used, then work out why each ingredient has been included – remember there are physical, sensory and nutritional functions. Look at the example in the table, which shows the function of ingredients in carrot and coriander soup.

Ingredient	Function
Carrot	Vitamin A
Potato	Thickener
Onion	Flavour
Coriander	Colour
Water	Bulk
Salt	Preservative
Pepper	Spiciness

Use books, your knowledge and experience, information from your teacher and a nutritional program to help you. Try to think of a different function for each ingredient if you can.

Extra ingredients

For the example of carrot and coriander soup, you could also write a list of extra ingredients, such as vegetables, which could be added to the product, listing their properties. For example:

- peppers = different colours = sweeten when cooked = high in vitamin C
- oranges = tangy flavour = high in vitamin C
- tomatoes = bright colour = sweet flavour = high in vitamin C.

To gain more marks, you should try and identify ingredients that will add different properties – mentioning vitamin C three times will only get you one mark, not three.

Experimenting with prototypes

You could spend at least one practical session experimenting with making prototypes. This work helps you to consider how initial design ideas can be developed into final products. Alternatively, you could think back to the work you did in your coursework and work out on paper how you would develop these products.

For example:

For the research context and design theme 'Outdoor entertaining, savoury products', you could make prototypes of burgers, kebabs using different vegetables and marinades for kebabs.

For example:

For the research context and design theme 'Food products for special occasions', you could experiment with different decorative finishes to cakes (different types of icing, use of cream, piping or modelling icing) or make prototypes of savoury pies or quiches.

For example:

For the research context and design theme 'Multicultural, ready-prepared vegetable products', you could make prototypes of vegetable burritos.

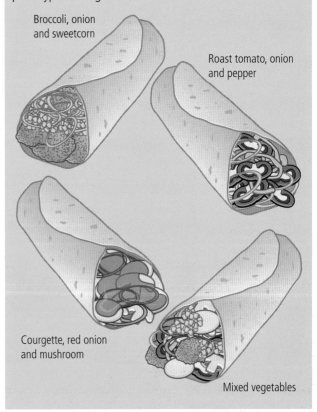

Broccoli, onion and sweetcorn

Roast tomato, onion and pepper

Courgette, red onion and mushroom

Mixed vegetables

Summary

★ Practical experience of the products identified in the preparation sheet is essential.

In this chapter you will:

★ learn about exam technique.

Good preparation for the food technology exam involves revision of the syllabus and practising exam technique for the different types of questions you will be asked.

As part of this preparation, you need to understand exam vocabulary.

Exam vocabulary

Compare You are expected to analyse the similarities and differences between two or more objects.

Describe This means to give an idea of something by specifying its nature or properties.

Develop This means to improve a basic idea. You will need to make changes and come up with a workable solution.

Evaluate This involves making judgements about something, often giving advantages and disadvantages.

Explain This usually requires reasons and depth about the subject.

Explain (or describe) in detail This requires a longer answer with more quality facts.

List This requires single words or phrases.

Name This is asking for the specific name of something. The examiner will want to see exact words, for example the name of a sensory test.

Use notes and sketches The answer must include diagrams. Full marks will not be awarded if only notes or sketches are used.

When you sit the exam, it is a good idea to read through the whole paper before you answer any questions. The paper follows the design process.

The first question or questions are usually about gathering and using information. Remember to read the questions carefully and look at the marks available.

Exam Hint
The top of each page identifies what the questions are about.

Question

Describe two ways a computer can be used to find out information about burger products.

(2 marks for each answer)

(AQA 2003)

'Using the Internet' would get only one mark.

'Using the Internet to look at and compare existing products' would gain the full two marks.

The design question

The next question is usually the design question. This is worth about one third of the exam marks. This question is usually divided into three sections.

Exam Hint
You can easily identify the design question as there will be a hint at the top of the page; for example, 'Question 2 is about designing new food products.'

Section 1

At the start of the design question, you are usually given design criteria. You will have used design criteria in your coursework to guide you with your ideas. Design criteria is another name for an outline specification, so you should be familiar with this. It is a list of things that the products should be like. Make sure you read the criteria carefully, then read it again!

You will then usually be asked to design two products that match this criteria. As part of your preparation for the exam, you need to practise for this design question by practising designing products similar to those you have had practical experience of making. Learn to draw in 3D, as a cross-section, or as a bird's eye view, whichever is appropriate. Add lots of detail so that it is clear what the illustration is and what ingredients it includes. Annotate (label) it and include a title. Specify the dimensions (height, width, diameter, and so on) and then add colour. However, remember that this section is usually worth 8–10 marks, so do not spend too long on it.

Section 2

For the next part of the design question, you will usually have to choose one of these designs as a final idea and justify your choice. You will have done this during your coursework. Explain why it is a good idea and how it meets the design criteria.

You might then be asked to write a product specification for this chosen product. Remember that a product specification includes more precise detail than an outline specification or design criteria. For example, 'Served in individual portions' in the list of design criteria could change to 'Each individual portion is 15cm diameter' in the product specification. Practise justifying an idea against the design criteria and writing a product specification for it.

Question

a Choose one of your ideas for the manufacturer to develop. Explain in detail how your chosen idea meets the design criteria.

(4 marks)

b Write a product specification for your chosen design idea.

(5 marks)

(AQA 2004)

Summary

★ Practise drawing products and writing specifications for them.

★ Memorise recipes.

★ Practise writing methods of making, including quality controls.

Section 3

You are then usually asked to show how your chosen product could be made.

Question

a List the ingredients needed to make your chosen design idea in the test kitchen. Explain the function of each ingredient.

(10 marks)

b Produce a plan for making your chosen idea in the test kitchen. Include details of:
   • two critical control points (CCPs) used
   • two examples of feedback given after control checks.
   You may use flow charts, diagrams, notes or sketches in your answer.

(8 marks)

(AQA 2004)

Practise by writing a list of the ingredients of the products you have made during your preparation based on the preparation sheet. Include quantities and the functions of each ingredient. Do this for at least two or three suitable products. You will not know exactly what the design criteria will be, so you must be familiar with a variety of products. For example, with the design theme of 'ready-prepared vegetable products', you might be asked to design a snack product, a side dish or a microwaveable ready meal.

The next thing you must practise is writing the method of production as if you were making it in a test kitchen or as if it were being mass produced. When writing the method, you should mention quality controls, including a HACCP plan.

Exam Hint
Use any relevant technical terms you know such as 'coagulates', 'foams' and 'bulking'.

If you are asked for a flow chart or procedure for making your product, including health and safety, you will not be awarded marks for repetition. You will only be awarded a mark the first time you mention a point.

Exam technique: How to maximise your marks

Once you have tackled the design question, the rest of the questions on the exam paper follow the stages in the design process: development of products, industrial processes, including health and safety, packaging and broader issues such as ethical issues.

Every question and subsection gives the marks that will be awarded in brackets in the right-hand column.

Lower-mark questions

Even when there are just two marks awarded, you need to think about how you can achieve both those marks.

> **Question**
>
> Barbecue products use many high-risk foods. Explain what is meant by a high-risk food.
>
> *(2 marks)*
>
> (AQA 2003)

If you answered, **'They are foods that are most likely to cause food poisoning'**, you would gain only one mark. If you added depth by saying, **'They are foods that are most likely to cause food poisoning because bacteria grow easily on them'**, you would gain two marks. You might also gain two marks by including two simplistic points such as, **'They are foods that are most likely to cause food poisoning and are foods high in protein.'** Other answers could include: high in moisture, and other explanations of storage and temperature.

In questions where four, five or six marks are given, you need to think about the points you will include and the detail you need to add to these points so you can get full marks. The answers you give should be extended writing. You could always make notes in pencil to the left or below the question before you start to write your full answer so that you remember what you want to include.

Your answer could include the range of healthy options

> **Question**
>
> Many consumers prefer healthier-option products. How does the range of barbecue products on sale offer healthier options to consumers?
>
> *(6 marks)*
>
> (AQA 2003)

available, such as high fibre, low or reduced fat, and how these are healthier options. Your answer could also include the risks of some foods and nutrients to your health; for example, **'Salt can cause high blood pressure.'**

This answer would get four marks as it is detailed about

> **Sample answer A**
>
> **'You can buy low-fat burgers, which means they may be less likely to cause obesity and heart disease. Vegetarian burgers are also better for you as they have less fat in them. They also have lots of vitamins and minerals. Many other barbecue products are low in fat. There is a good range of ready-made salads with low-fat dressings, so these are healthy, too, as they also contain vitamins and minerals. Barbecuing is better than frying as the fat drips away from the food rather than being absorbed into it.'**

low-fat products and identifies the higher vitamin content of vegetables. However, it does not cover a wide range of related issues to gain higher marks.

This answer covers fat, salt, fibre, sugar and extra vitamins,

> **Sample answer B**
>
> **'There are all sorts of healthy-option barbecue products available. In fact, barbecuing itself is good as it is more like grilling than frying as the fat drips off the food. Some burgers are low fat and this would lower the risk of obesity and heart disease. You can also get 100% beef burgers that do not have any extra salt in them – too much salt in the diet can cause high blood pressure. Kebabs are made with lean meat such as chicken. Bread products that are eaten with barbecued meat can be wholemeal so**

have a higher fibre (NSP) content. Fibre in foods prevents constipation and can lower the risk of some cancers. Salads that are served with meat also contain fibre, vitamins and minerals, so these are healthy. There are a lot of low-fat salad dressings and you can even buy reduced-sugar ketchup to use. Vegetarian burgers are good as they are low in fat and full of fibre and vitamins. So, there are lots of healthier-option products available.'

and gives examples of each kind of product. Therefore it would be awarded the full six marks.

> **Exam Hint** You do not need to include six individual points as these mid-range questions are also marked against the following criteria:
> - 1–2 marks shows a simplistic answer showing some understanding
> - 3–4 marks shows a number of simplistic answers or one detailed answer showing understanding of several aspects
> - 5–6 marks shows good communication of a wide range of related issues and relevant examples.

Higher-mark questions

If you are taking the higher-mark paper, there will be more higher-mark, extended writing questions. Therefore, you need to practise the technique of writing longer answers, which include arguments. Some questions can be worth ten or twelve marks, so you need to be organised and skilled in the way you answer them. You might approach such a question in three steps:

1 Underline or highlight the key words or sections in the question.

Question

Explain what is meant by the term 'organic vegetables'. Give reasons why organic vegetables are becoming more popular with consumers.

(7 marks)

(AQA 2004)

2 Using a pencil, in the margin or at the bottom of the page, make notes on the points you want to include in your answer. Do the points cover all the key sections? Are there enough points here to help you gain full marks? Can you explain some of the points in detail to gain more marks? Make sure that if a question is asking for arguments for and against an issue you give both – otherwise you will lose marks.

3 Only now should you start to write your full answer. You should have practised writing your answer on the question most likely to come up, as identified from the preparation sheet.

Question

Explain how manufacturers of barbecue food products are meeting the varying social, cultural and moral needs of consumers.

(12 marks)

(AQA 2003)

> **Exam Hint**
> - 1–3 marks shows basic knowledge of the product range and how it meets consumer needs.
> - 4–6 marks communicates reasonable knowledge of products and can relate some of these issues to consumer needs.
> - 7–8 marks communicates good knowledge of relevant products and can relate to different issues related to consumer needs.
> - 9–12 marks shows identification of needs through market/consumer research. Communicates sound knowledge of relevant products and can relate to a range of issues related to consumer

Sample answer A

'More barbecue products are being sold because people have more leisure time, but they have not been taught basic cooking skills so they want ready-made products. They want healthy products, so there are low-fat options available such as low-fat burgers. People also eat salads with their barbecue because vegetables are full of vitamins and this is good for you. Wholemeal bread can also be eaten as it contains fibre. Some people will not eat beef because of their religion, so lamb or chicken burgers are sold.'

This answer is not long enough to gain full marks. It shows reasonable knowledge, which is related to consumer needs, and gives one point relating to social, cultural and moral needs. This answer would get five marks.

This answer would gain full marks as it shows sound knowledge of a range of relevant products that relate to consumers' differing needs.

Sample answer B

'Consumer needs change over time. If manufacturers carry out research, such as questionnaires, they will find out want consumers want now. Today, we have more leisure time so we are more likely to have more barbecues, but many of us have less skills in preparing food so ready-prepared barbecue packs are becoming more popular. A lot of people are concerned about their health and want to eat low-fat, low-sugar and low-salt products, and foods high in fibre. There are a lot of healthy-option barbecue products available: 100% lean beef burgers are low in fat and low in salt, so are less likely to cause obesity or high blood pressure. Kebabs are also made with lean meat, often chicken. They also sometimes contain vegetables as well as meat, which are low in fat and full of vitamins. They also contain fibre, which prevents constipation and can prevent some cancers. Vegetarian burgers are just as healthy. Salads are served with barbecues and are full of good nutrients. They can be served with low-fat salad dressings.

Other barbecue products are organic because some people are concerned about fertilisers and pesticides used in conventional farming, and they are not sure of the long-term effects of genetically modified farming. They want to eat meat from animals that have been reared to organic standards.

The variety of barbecue products available reflects the multicultural society in which we live: Chinese spare ribs, tandoori chicken and kebabs from Mediterranean countries. These foods are also popular because we travel on holiday to these countries and try out different foods rather than just eating traditional foods. Some manufacturers also produce a range of barbeque products that do not include certain ingredients like pork or beef, which certain religions do not allow.

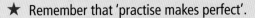

Summary

★ Remember that 'practise makes perfect'.

★ If you revise and practise answers for your food technology exam, you will enter the exam confident that you will do you best. You can do it! Good luck!

Glossary

Additives Substances added to foods in small amounts to perform a function such as to colour, flavour or preserve a product.

Attribute profile A diagram showing evaluation ratings for a specific product.

Batch production The production of a limited number of items.

Component A part of something (for example, mashed potato is a component of shepherd's pie).

Computer-aided design (CAD) Use of a computer program, such as a nutritional analysis program, to design a product.

Computer-aided manufacture (CAM) Use of a computer program, such as a meat depositor, to manufacture a product.

Concept screening Looking at lots of ideas and choosing the most suitable one.

Consumer Someone who buys or uses a product or service.

Cook-chill foods Foods that have been cooked, chilled quickly to below 5°C and then stored at a low temperature for reheating later.

Critical control points (CCPs) Stages in the production process that are checked regularly to make sure errors and risks are reduced.

Cross-contamination The transfer of a hazardous substance, such as bacteria, from one area to another.

Danger zone The temperature range in which bacteria thrive (5–63°C).

Diet The food and drink we eat.

Due diligence In food preparation this means that the company has set up systems to help avoid contamination of food products. They have done all they possibly can to avoid contamination.

E number The number given to an additive to show that it has been approved by the EU.

Feedback Used by control systems to see if the process is working correctly and if the output is correct.

Hazard Analysis Critical Control Points (HACCP) A system of identifying, assessing and controlling food safety hazards.

Hazard Anything that can cause harm to the consumer (physical, chemical and biological hazards).

High-risk area The section(s) in the food production process where food is most likely to be contaminated by bacteria.

High-risk foods Those most likely to encourage bacterial growth, foods high in protein.

Macronutrients Nutrients needed in large quantities by the body – protein, fat and carbohydrates.

Marketing Selling a product or service to a customer.

Mass production The production of a large number of items.

Micronutrients Nutrients, such as vitamins and minerals, which are needed in small quantities by the body.

Modelling To experiment with an idea without actually carrying it out – you can model the nutritional value of a food product.

Modified atmosphere packaging (MAP) Also called controlled atmosphere packaging, this packaging method extends shelf life by delaying the growth of bacteria.

Nutritional profile The make-up of a product from its nutritional content.

One-off production When one special product is made.

Organoleptic properties Sensory properties such as taste, texture and appearance.

Product range A range of products with the same name and basic ingredients, for example scones, sausages, pasta sauce.

Profit The difference between production costs and selling price.

Prototype The first version of a product, used for testing, development and evaluation.

Quality assurance A quality management system that is set up before a product is made, which lays down procedures for making a safe, quality product.

Quality control The steps in the process of making a product to make sure it meets the standards set.

Risk assessment Also called hazard analysis, this is the process of judging how likely a problem is to occur, using a low, medium and high scale.

Sensory descriptors Words that describe taste, smell, texture and flavour.

Sensory evaluation A way of describing the characteristics of a product using the senses such as smell, texture and flavour.

Sensory tests Tests on food products to find out the sensory characteristics, for example taste and smell.

Shelf life How long a food product can be kept, making sure it is safe to eat and good quality.

Smart ingredients Food ingredients that have been changed so that they behave in a certain way, for example Quorn is made to taste and feel like chicken, modified starches have been created so that they stay runny when chilled.

Specification A list of properties that a product or group of products must have – what it should be like.

System Made up of input, process, output and feedback.

Target group The person or group of people that the product is aimed at, for example children, coeliacs.

Tolerance level The amount of flexibility allowed when making a product – in terms of weight, colour, size – so that it meets quality standards.

Index